The Surrey Hills
40 *favourite walks*

CW01159796

The author and publisher have made every effort to ensure that the information in this publication is accurate, and accept no responsibility whatsoever for any loss, injury or inconvenience experienced by any person or persons whilst using this book.

published by
pocket mountains ltd
The Old Church, Annanside,
Moffat DG10 9HB

ISBN: 978-1-907025-969

Text and photography copyright © Ben Giles 2023

The right of Ben Giles to be identified as the Author of this work has been asserted by him in accordance with the Copyright, Designs and Patents Act 1988

A catalogue record for this book is available from the British Library

Contains Ordnance Survey data © Crown copyright and database 2023 supported by out of copyright mapping 1945-1961

All rights reserved. No part of this publication may be reproduced, stored in a retrieval system, or transmitted in any form or by any means, electronic or mechanical, including photocopying and recording, unless expressly permitted by Pocket Mountains Ltd.

Printed by J Thomson Colour Printers, Glasgow

Introduction

A little over 100 years ago, the writer Edward Thomas passed through the Surrey Hills on his journey by bicycle from London to the Quantocks. In the opening chapters of *In Pursuit of Spring*, his account of that Easter journey in March 1913, he describes how, leaving London behind, he pedals for Epsom and then for Leatherhead, beyond which the River Mole takes him through the gap in the North Downs past Mickleham and Box Hill to Dorking. Departing from the description of his route, he turns to reflect upon 'the poet naturally thought of here': George Meredith.

A detour follows on the 'joy of woods and fields' and, in passing, Thomas conjures up the presence of other literary lights – Wordsworth, W H Hudson, Shelley, Shakespeare, Byron and George Borrow. But 'Meredith of Box Hill' he sees not just as a lover of nature, like other poets, but one tempered by the Surrey landscape itself and above all as one 'fit to be ranked with the whitebeam, the lark and the southwest wind'. As Thomas wheeled along, one of Meredith's poems he had in mind was *The Lark Ascending*, set the following year to music by Ralph Vaughan Williams, another artist who was intimately connected with the county and whose family home was nearby at Leith Hill Place.

Onward went the would-be poet Thomas that blustery Good Friday through the villages and commons of Westcott, Wotton, Gomshall and Shere. Criss-crossing the tiny Tillingbourne he passes under the shadow of St Martha's Church, high on its steep hill above Chilworth. Here his mood changes and he shudders at the gunpowder mills, 'something inhuman, diabolical', but his spirits are raised by the sight of a ridge bristling westwards on the far side of Guildford, the Hog's Back. On its height is the high road that will take him to Farnham and beyond, a route which he thinks of as fit for the gods 'because it is as much in heaven as on earth'.

Any Edwardian nowadays finding themselves following this same route over the Hog's Back by bike or on foot would be forgiven for thinking they had entered on a highway to hell, transformed as it is from Thomas' majestic, dusty road to the thunderous dual carriageways of the A31, something he would no doubt have also found inhuman and diabolical. But for all the differences, the undulating crest still gives, in essence, the same view out over the same hills, woods and heaths, though inevitably changed by a century in which Greater London has expanded into what was northern Surrey, and the towns and villages in the folds of its valleys have become more populous and ever more frequented by people seeking open spaces and fresher air.

What might also surprise those earlier generations of pioneering ramblers, romantics and enthusiasts of the outdoors is the level of protection now afforded this landscape. In 1958 much of the area of the chalk North Downs running from Farnham in the west to Oxted in the east and the Greensand Ridge stretching from Haslemere to its high point on Leith Hill was included in the Surrey Hills Area of Outstanding Natural Beauty (AONB), now a landscape with status equivalent to a national park. This guarantee of protection covers over a quarter of the whole county and within its boundaries are to be found some of the most accessible and sought-after green spaces in South East England.

About this guide
This guide contains 40 circular routes ranging in length from a short stroll of one hour to half a day's walk, divided into five sections broadly based on the topography and boundaries of the Surrey Hills AONB. Most of the routes are intended as comfortable walks and the majority can be completed inside two or three hours, while there are a few longer or more strenuous routes, especially those that venture over higher ground. In general the walking is on well-worn paths, lanes and tracks, with plenty of waymarks to help with route finding. The route descriptions concentrate on the salient points of navigation, but may not cover every twist and turn. If in doubt the obvious path is usually the line to take. In addition, the accompanying sketch maps serve an illustrative purpose and – for the longer or more complex routes – it would be a good idea to have access to the relevant OS Explorer mapping, details of which are given at the start of each walk.

The Surrey Hills themselves are a compact but varied area. At their western end lies the busy town of Farnham, famous for its castle and Georgian streetscape with its open heaths stretching southwards past Frensham Ponds to Hindhead and The Devil's Punch Bowl. Eastwards the villages of Seale, Puttenham and Shackleford with their fields, woods and parkland below the ridge of the Hog's Back bring you to the busy A3, now finally rerouted underground through tunnels beneath Gibbet Hill. Haslemere and Godalming enclose an area of rolling countryside and pretty villages spread around and over the Greensand Ridge, with the county border of Sussex just to the south. Here, old industries such as glass, iron and charcoal-making and the arrival of the railway had transformed the area long before the advent of modern commuting and tourism.

Moving eastwards, Guildford – in medieval times the county capital and now its second most populous town – dominates the central area. Here are to be found the well-known villages of Chilworth, Shere, and Gomshall alongside the gentle Tilling Bourne. Beyond, the higher ground of Hurtwood Common, with its secluded, if highly popular, villages of Holmbury St Mary and Peaslake, gives long views from its southern escarpment over the Low Weald and beyond to the South Downs. Next in line to the east is Dorking and some of the best known and most visited parts of the Surrey Hills. The town of Leatherhead lies to the north through the famous gap in the North Downs, cut by the River Mole on its way to the Thames. Dorking itself is surrounded by the high ground of Box Hill, Ranmore Common and Leith Hill, its iconic tower topping the second highest point in the South East.

The final, most easterly section is centred on the town of Reigate. Here the proximity of London most keenly imposes its presence on the Surrey Hills. The orbital M25 carves its most southerly track here, intersected by the M23 on its way to Sussex and the coast. The older line of the A25 still gives the easiest access to many of the villages hereabouts, including Skimmington, Godstone and Limpsfield, while a pocket of the AONB away to the southeast near the county border with Kent has some easily-overlooked countryside around Lingfield and Dormansland.

Getting around and access

The main towns of the Surrey Hills are Farnham, Haslemere, Godalming, Dorking, Reigate, Redhill and Oxted. All benefit from regular bus routes and railway stations, making the Surrey Hills well-placed for travel by public transport. There are direct trains from London Victoria and Waterloo and many of the villages between the main towns can be accessed by rail. An effort has been made to start walks from places served by public transport and it is usually possible to plan the completion of a walk from a town to coincide with train times. However, some of the more secluded areas and villages of the Surrey Hills are only intermittently served by public buses on both a weekly and seasonal basis.

Access by car is still the preferred option for many, and while towns cater adequately for parking, this can be a sensitive issue in villages. An indication has been given where possible of parking options but it is very common in popular spots for all parking space to be filled early in the day, especially at weekends and during peak holiday season. Many of the routes are set relatively close together and it should be possible to amend plans and choose an alternative walk should parking be unavailable.

Despite its being one of the most populous counties with more than one million inhabitants, there is still plenty of farming to be found, mostly arable and some dairy and sheep. Local signs may indicate the need to keep dogs on a lead and dogs can be a problem for cows, especially if they have recently calved or been let out of winter sheds. If in doubt, it is usually advisable and possible to find a short detour.

Farnham is the westernmost town in Surrey. It sits in the valley of the River Wey near the western limit of the North Downs and the county border with Hampshire. It is equally well known for its castle, Bishop's Palace and medieval deer park as it is for its Georgian townhouses, busy streets and shops. It also has a long-feted association with the radical politician, soldier and reformer William Cobbett, author of *Rural Rides*, who was born here in 1763.

Along the River Wey to the southeast stand the ruins of Waverley Abbey, established by Cistercian monks from France in the 12th century. To the north of the line of the current B3001 lies an area of rolling countryside of fields and woods which meets the steep escarpment of the ridge of the Hog's Back. Here are found the still peaceful, if popular, villages of Seale, Puttenham and Shackleford, with the parkland of Peper Harow nearby.

South of the B3001 and the River Wey the land gradually rises and is dominated by the ancient heaths around Frensham and its ponds. In a triangulating pincer movement towards Hindhead, the A287 to the west and the main artery of the A3 to the east enclose the highest ground around the Devil's Punch Bowl, though the latter road no longer passes over the head of this magnificent combe but is buried in tunnels below.

Farnham and the west

1 Farnham Park and Castle 8
Tread in the footsteps of the Bishops of Winchester on this easy parkland circuit

2 Crooksbury Hill and Waverley Abbey 10
Explore country lanes, bridleways and the ruins of a once-substantial abbey founded by the 'white monks'

3 Seale 12
Set out from this handsome village for a short wander through woodland and fields at the foot of the Hog's Back

4 Puttenham Common 14
Enjoy a circuit on bridleways and woodland paths around one of the county's most popular commons

5 Shackleford and Peper Harow Park 16
Combine two short but varied loops around parkland surrounding a pair of charming villages

6 Tilford and Frensham Little Pond 18
Don't forget to pack binoculars for this river- and pond-side stroll through wildlife-rich countryside

7 Frensham Great Pond 20
Although a popular spot, it's easy to leave the crowds behind on this waterside and woodland circular

8 Churt and Whitmoor Vale 22
Follow the old route from London, passing old mills along the way

9 Gibbet Hill and the Devil's Punch Bowl 24
One of Surrey's classic walks through National Trust-managed woodland

FARNHAM AND THE WEST

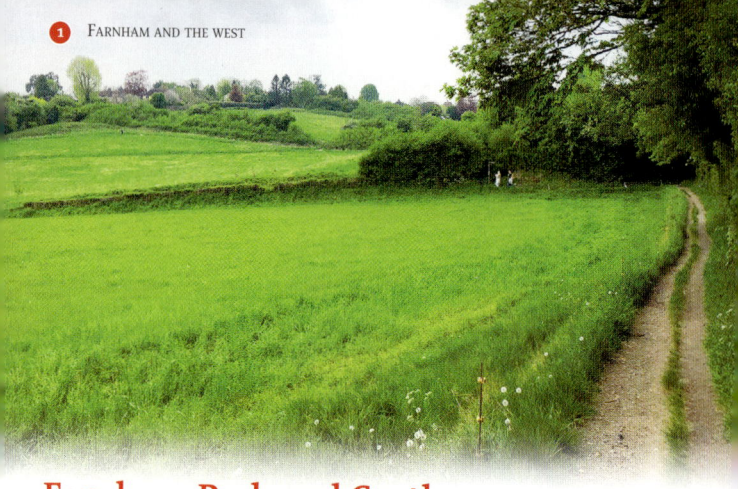

Farnham Park and Castle

Distance 6km **Time** 1 hour 30
Terrain parkland, woods and fields
Map OS Explorer 145 **Access** bus to
Farnham Park from Guildford,
Godalming and Hindhead; trains from
Guildford to Farnham Station, 1km
from the start

Visit a medieval park before enjoying the open countryside to the west of the historic town of Farnham.

Farnham Park has a history stretching back to the 14th century when it was enclosed to serve as a deer park for the Bishops of Winchester, but there is evidence that the site has been occupied by humans for at least 7000 years. Farnham Castle, in origin a Norman motte and bailey, is located in the southwestern corner of the park and can be visited at the start or end of the walk. There is free entry to the keep, which has good views over the town and park, and to an exhibition detailing the castle's history. Guided tours are available to the adjacent Tudor and Restoration buildings of the Bishop's Palace.

The walk starts from Farnham Park car park up Castle Hill to the north of Farnham town centre. From the car park head into Farnham Park away from the cricket ground and castle on a tarmac path for 200m past Park Café and the golf course clubhouse to a path junction. A left turn takes you northwards through the centre of the park down across the dip of Swallow Hole in woodland and up the rise ahead into open parkland.

Continue over the crosspaths down to the Nadder Stream, beyond which a short pull brings you up to the north end of the park. The route continues left down into

FARNHAM PARK AND CASTLE

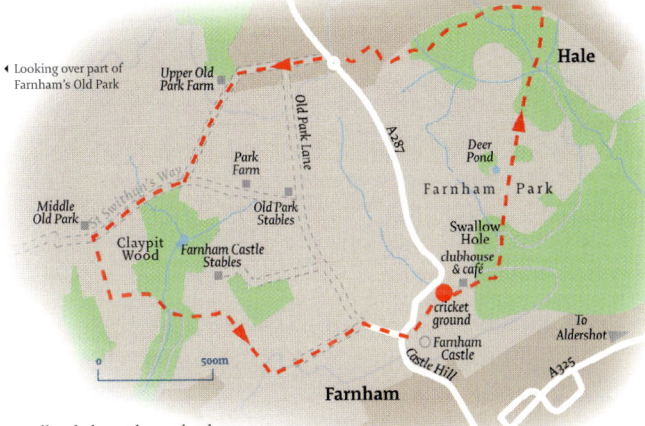

◀ Looking over part of Farnham's Old Park

woodland along the park edge on an undulating path for 500m to a stream. The main path bends right here, but keep ahead over the stream, out of the woodland and up the rise ahead to a crossbench and look out for the walkway off to the right at the park entrance by houses. Bear right along the walkway into the housing estate and turn left along Hampton Road to the junction, then left again up to the roundabout and the A287.

A dogleg right for 50m, then left takes you onto Upper Old Park Lane, a gravel track which heads past houses and over Old Park Lane to a junction. Here, you bear left onto a bridleway track down past Upper Old Park Farm and along the track between fields, where the views open out, to a path junction by a house.

The route now turns right onto the waymarked St Swithun's Way down into woodland, across a dip with a stream and up a line of pollarded oaks to a lane at a bend, 30m beyond which a left turn through a gate takes you into fields. Follow the footpath which heads along the left-hand edge of the first small field, across the second, and left along the edge of the third down into woodland. Cross the stream at the bottom and head uphill for 200m to a gate out of the trees, after which the path bends right and descends gently down the valley between fields for 300m to a crosspaths. A left turn along the field edge takes you alongside a hedge up to Old Park Lane. Turn right for 200m to reach the A287, across which you can detour downhill to the right to the entrance to Farnham Castle. To return to the start, once across the road, turn left up the walkway alongside the castle moat to the cricket club and car park beyond.

9

Crooksbury Hill and Waverley Abbey

Distance 7.5km **Time** 2 hours
Terrain lanes, woodland paths and fields
Map OS Explorer 145 **Access** no public transport to the start

Step back into the past on this route to an ancient hillfort and ruined abbey beside the River Wey.

Start from the upper part of The Sands on Littleworth Road at the junction with The Green and Smugglers Way by the Barley Mow pub, where there is some roadside parking or the pub car park is available for those visiting the pub.

Waverley Abbey was established by Cistercian monks in the 12th century and it was the first foundation of their order in England. Even though the abbey buildings are now ruins it is still easy to gauge just by wandering around how substantial the place once was. The 'white monks' who founded Waverley came from Aumone in Normandy, but followed the main precept of their chief abbey at Citeaux in Burgundy that their religious houses were not to be located 'in cities, castles, or villages, but in places remote from the conversation of men'. The secluded setting by the River Wey is also reminiscent of other Cistercian houses, such as Tintern and Fountains Abbey. As elsewhere, the monks of Waverley were involved in the wool trade and as their profits increased, so too did the abbey's buildings. They also built bridges at Tilford and Eashing, still in use today.

Head up Smugglers Way past the pub for 250m and take the bridleway off right into woodland, After 150m fork left onto a path over Soldiers Ring, a late Bronze or early Iron Age hillfort. On the far side of the earthworks beyond a wooden barrier a path heads steeply up to the top of Crooksbury Hill, where a topograph points out the views southwards to Gibbet Hill and Butser Hill. To descend, take the path

CROOKSBURY HILL AND WAVERLEY ABBEY

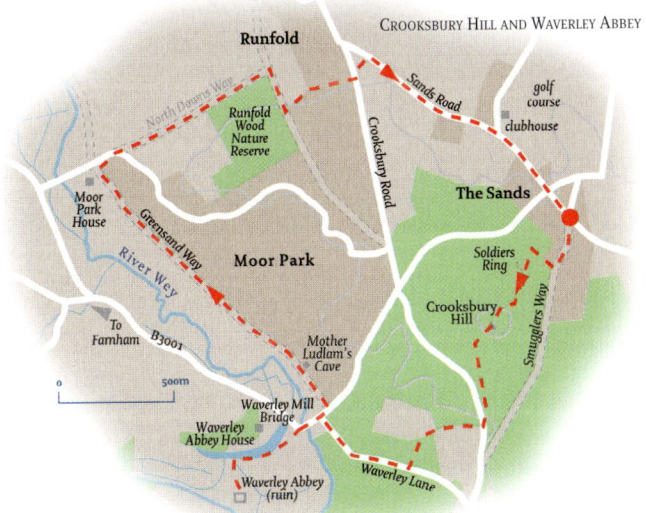

immediately beyond the topograph, down steps to the car park below.

Here, a path leads off left through the woodland, downhill and parallel to the road for 100m to meet a bridleway. Bear right to the road, across which the bridleway continues down a rough lane past cottages to Waverley Lane. A right turn down this wide lane takes you to the bend by Waverley Mill Bridge, where you can detour left for 500m over the River Wey to visit the ruins of Waverley Abbey across the water meadows beyond. A number of information boards help to interpret the site.

The onward route doglegs right, then left to continue for the next 1.5km along the route of the Greensand Way past Stella Cottage and into Moor Park, passing Mother Ludlam's Cave, former abode of a legendary white witch, before emerging from the trees to reach the gated Moor Park House.

Just before the gates at Moor Park House keep an eye out for the marker post for the North Downs Way which heads off right over a stile and steeply up Compton Way. Round the bend, look out for the North Downs Way markers off left and follow the trail between fields before passing into Runfold Wood Nature Reserve to reach a bridleway junction. Turn right for 150m, then left to stay on the North Downs Way, which now passes along the backs of houses, doglegs left, then right across Crooksbury Road and heads along a short section of footpath to emerge onto Sands Road. Turn right for just over 1km along the road over the rise into The Sands, past Farnham Golf Club, where the North Downs Way heads off left, and back up to the start.

◀ The ruins of Waverley Abbey

Seale

Distance 3km **Time** 1 hour
Terrain lanes, fields and woodland paths
Map OS Explorer 145 **Access** no public transport to the start

Take a short stroll from a lovely village at the foot of the Hog's Back escarpment, favoured by walkers and cyclists.

The walk starts from the centre of the village of Seale by Manor Farm, where there is a craft centre and tearoom in the 17th- and 18th-century courtyard buildings. Some parking is available in the courtyard and also on Wood Lane.

Walk up past the Church of St Laurence, where you will find an old wooden clarinet, a 15th-century will, many Woodroffe family plaques and some interesting windows. Opposite the war memorial, turn sharp right up School Hill past cottages, the Old Post Office and the village hall to rejoin Elstead Road higher up. Turn right along the pavement round the bend and then take the North Downs Way off left into woodland.

The path heads along the edge of the trees at the rear of gardens for 300m, before doglegging left to a gate and then continuing to the right into fields. Follow the right-hand field edge for 300m to a gate where you can enjoy good views down the valley and up to the Hog's Back. At the gate turn left onto a waymarked permissive path (courtesy of the Hampton Estate) down the field alongside the fence to a stile. Head into the Scots pine woodland beyond and after 50m, at the marker post, bear right down across the small dip to Puttenham Road.

Across the road a footpath goes through a tall gate, then alongside deer fencing and the backs of gardens and over a

◀ Bluebell woods near Seale

stream before climbing the hillside. These wooded slopes are carpeted in bluebells in springtime. The path winds its way uphill along the backs of more gardens to a top gate into a field. Bear left along the field edge, then keep on along a fenced pathway. The climb soon steepens, but before long you reach the top of Wood Lane just below the A31, which runs along the top of the Hog's Back.

A left turn down Wood Lane for 600m takes you past Seale Chalk Pit. You can make a short detour off to the right to the pit which, until the first part of the 20th century, provided quicklime for fields and mortar for building – it is now a Site of Special Scientific Interest notable for its rare chalkland plants and flowers. Carry on down the lane with views over the village to return to the start.

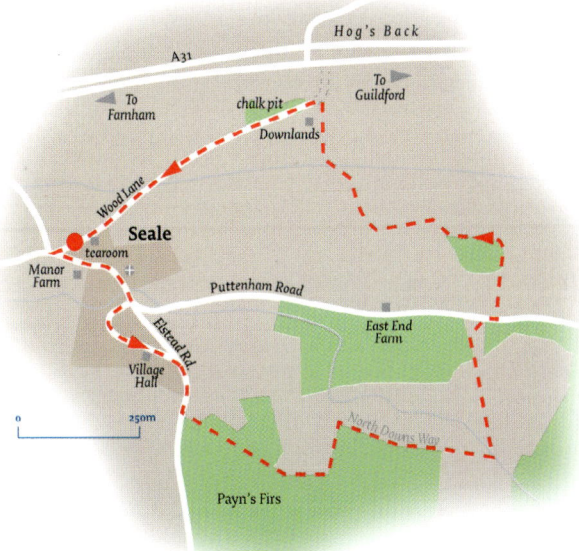

13

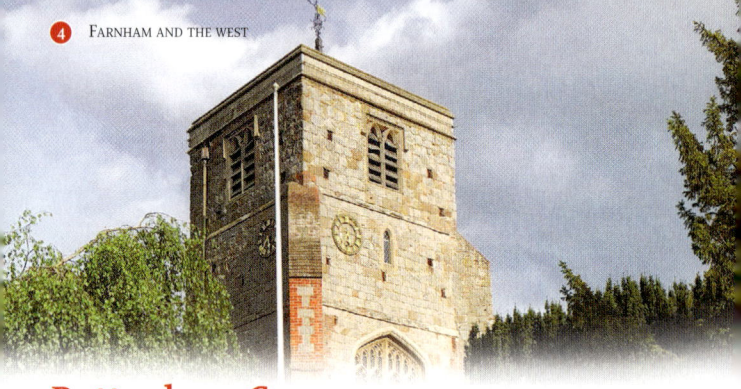

Puttenham Common

Distance 8km **Time** 2 hours 15
Terrain lanes, open common and fields
Map OS Explorer 145 **Access** bus to
Puttenham Crossroads from Guildford
and Farnham stops on the Hog's Back
(A31), 500m from the start

This varied walk explores one of Surrey's most popular commons, with fine views.

The walk starts from the village of Puttenham, where there is some roadside parking on The Street. An alternative start is at Puttenham Middle car park on Suffield Lane, halfway along the route.

Puttenham is a delightful village situated below the Hog's Back. The houses along The Street are a varied mix of brick, sandstone and chalk. At the east end are the war memorial and the Church of St John the Baptist, which has an old village well just inside the gate. This had been filled in during the 1700s but was rediscovered in 1972 when, to the surprise of churchgoers on Palm Sunday, a tree collapsed downwards into it. The large house to the south of the church is Puttenham Priory, which was originally known as the Manor House and dates from the 13th century. It was remodelled in the second half of the 18th century in Palladian style by Thomas Parker. Its previous owner was General James Oglethorpe, founder of the American colony of Georgia, and it is thought that General's Pond on Puttenham Heath is named after him.

Walk along The Street past The Good Intent pub up to the west end of the village and bear left along Lascombe Lane. After 100m keep right along the North Downs Way which leads uphill and then winds up past Lascombe House, designed by Edwin Lutyens. It emerges on Puttenham Common itself before heading downhill to the small parking area at Totford Hatch.

Here, turn left off the North Downs Way onto the bridleway which climbs gently southwards for 400m to a bridleway junction with a marker post, where you

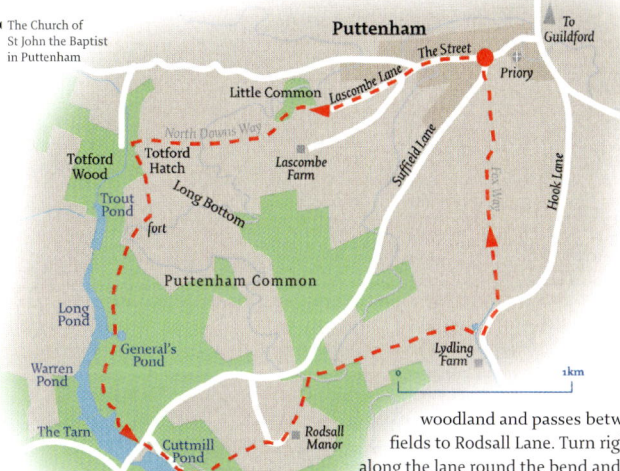

◀ The Church of St John the Baptist in Puttenham

bear right up to the site of Hillbury hillfort. Keep on over the level area and make your way a little down the slope beyond to a bridleway junction and marker post. Fork right onto the bridleway heading downhill through woodland for 500m to General's Pond. At the bridleway junction beyond, bear right to continue through the woodland to a small stream by The Tarn pond. Fork right to the pond and then left along the water's-edge path to Suffield Lane. (A left fork at the stream takes you to Puttenham Middle car park.)

Head across the road and along Cutt Mill Lane beside the pond before bearing left along the drive. Continue past Cutt Mill House and up to Willow Cottage, after which a bridleway heads up into the woodland and passes between fields to Rodsall Lane. Turn right along the lane round the bend and up past Rodsall Manor and cottages, beyond which the bridleway heads up a wooded holloway for 300m to a staggered crosspaths. A right turn here takes you for the next 1km between plantations and then fields where the footpath starts to descend gently, before bending right past a small pond to reach Puttenham Lane.

Turn left up the lane for 150m and, before the bend, take the footpath off left onto the route of the Fox Way for the next 1.3km. This footpath heads up the narrow field ahead before climbing a steep bank and passing along a wide fenced pathway between more fields and over a rise, with good views to the Hog's Back. From here, you descend gently into woodland and along a hedged section to reach Suffield Lane, where a right turn takes you past the entrance to Puttenham Priory and back into the village.

Shackleford and Peper Harow Park

Distance 3.5km or 5.5km **Time** 1 hour or 1 hour 30 **Terrain** lanes, parkland and woods **Map** OS Explorer 145 **Access** bus to Shackleford from Farnham and Godalming

A picturesque route leads from one of Surrey's prettiest villages with an option of an extended loop through woods.

The walk starts from the centre of the village of Shackleford, where there is a post office, village shop and a small car park opposite the bus stop. The unusual name of Peper Harow is thought to originate from an 11th-century estate owner called Pepard. The parish was known as Pipereheargae in Norman times and this provides the possibility of an alternative interpretation. The Old English word *hearge* means 'temple' or 'altar' and has given rise to the notion that hereabouts stood a Temple of the Pipers. Following this, some have even suggested the name might refer to the presence of a Roman temple, though none has been unearthed. Peper Harow Park is a delight to wander through and was laid out in its current form in the 18th century by Lancelot 'Capability' Brown, when the old manor house was replaced with the current Peper Harow House, seat of the Lords Midleton until the 20th century. Cricket has been played in the park since the 1720s, though the house itself has now been converted into apartments.

Walk up Peper Harow Lane for 600m past The Cyder House Inn and cricket field and up alongside Shackleford Heath. Take the bridleway off left along the line of telegraph poles to the southeast corner of the heath. Across Elstead Road the bridleway continues along a woodland strip for 500m to a crosspaths. A right turn takes you into parkland, over the shoulder of the rise ahead and down past the cricket field to the buildings of Peper

SHACKLEFORD AND PEPER HAROW PARK

◀ The village sign and Shackleford Post Office

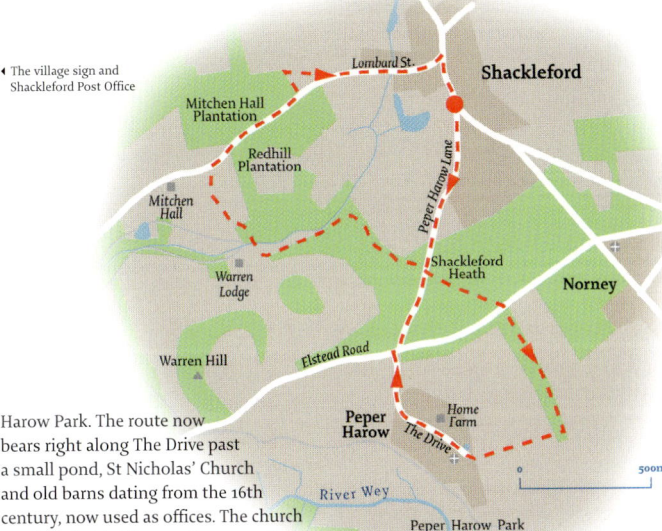

Harow Park. The route now bears right along The Drive past a small pond, St Nicholas' Church and old barns dating from the 16th century, now used as offices. The church was founded in Norman times on what in origin may be a Saxon foundation but has an unusual mix of English 'medieval' styles, which surprisingly date only from the middle of the 19th century, when the Midleton family commissioned Augustus Pugin to redesign the building. The old yew which stands in the churchyard is estimated to be more than 1000 years old.

At the bend bear right with The Drive up to Elstead Road, where a dogleg right, then left takes you back along Peper Harow Lane. After 300m at the bridleway crosspaths you can choose to head straight back down into Shackleford or follow the second loop.

For the second loop, turn left onto the bridleway, which winds its way down the edge of the woodland, before turning left at the bottom and heading straight for the cottages at Warren Lodge. Here, bear right and follow the bridleway as it twists its way up to Lombard Street.

Turn right and follow the narrow lane with care through the bends, over the rise and down to a byway junction after 450m. Turn left up the byway for 100m to the left-hand bend. Here, turn right into the field to take a footpath descending to a gate back onto Lombard Street. Turn left along the road into Shackleford to the junction, where a right turn will take you back along The Street to the centre of the village.

17

6 FARNHAM AND THE WEST

Tilford and Frensham Little Pond

Distance 7.5km (with option of 2.5km extension around Little Pond)
Time 2 hours (extra 45 mins for extension) **Terrain** bridleways, lanes and woodland paths **Map** OS Explorer 145
Access no public transport to the start

This longer approach to the smaller of Frensham's famous ponds via Tancred's ford is well worth the effort.

The walk starts from the village of Tilford, known for its cricket ground on The Green and the Barley Mow pub. The famous Tilford Oak stands on the north side of The Green, now battened with metal plates but still grand nonetheless. Opposite, at the northwestern corner of The Green, is a younger oak planted in 1902 to commemorate the coronation of Edward VII, while the tree at the southern corner has been grown from an acorn of the one toppled in the great storm of 1987. Tilford also has two bridges, originally built at the direction of the monks of Waverley Abbey in the late 13th century. The river here, known locally as the Till, is the southern branch of the River Wey and flows in from the southwest under the West Bridge to meet the northern branch of the Wey in the water meadow behind the Barley Mow pub, before the combined stream passes under the arches of the East Bridge. There is parking by The Green and a car park on its east side. If full, an alternative is to start the walk from Frensham Little Pond, where there is a car park.

From The Green go over the East Bridge and turn left onto the bridleway alongside the water meadows of the River Wey up to the junction with the byway of Squires Hill Lane. Bear left up the byway to the top of the rise and, at the fork beyond, keep left onto a bridleway, down across a track and up a small rise, before a steep descent to Sheephatch Lane at Tilfordmill Bridge. A left turn down this lane leads over the River Wey to Tilford Road after 500m. Cross the road and take the bridleway up into the wooded Farnham Heath Nature Reserve. The bridleway soon

TILFORD AND FRENSHAM LITTLE POND

◀ Looking over Frensham Little Pond

bears left on an undulating path for just under 500m to meet The Reeds Road at a sharp right-hand bend.

Cross the road and continue along the bridleway to Tilford Reeds, down past houses and then along an undulating fenced track for the next 1km over Tankersford Common, an RSPB reserve, before bending left down past the Verdun Chestnuts to Pierrepoint Home Farm. Here, bear left past the Old Dairy and keep on to Tancred's ford and bridge over the River Wey. On the right is Wey Meadow, now protected as a Site of Special Scientific Interest. In the 16th century it saw a pioneering project engineered by Rowland Vaughan from Herefordshire's Golden Valley for deliberately flooding the area by means of sluices and channels to encourage the growth of grass for cattle to graze on at the end of winter, a perennial worry for farmers.

The bridleway now heads uphill and into woodland to a junction with a byway, where a dogleg left for 20m, then right takes you over Priory Lane to the entrance to Frensham Little Pond. This was formed in the 13th century, a generation after its larger neighbour, to increase the stock of fish for the bishops at Farnham. Now there is the Tern Café with its bird-hide telescope and you can extend the route by following the waymarked path for 2.5km around the pond to spot wildlife.

The return route retraces steps over Priory Lane to the byway and turns right along the wide sandy track, across a dip and then past Chuter's Firs and a path in from the right. Just over 150m beyond this, fork left onto a footpath which takes you down past the buildings of Meadow End Farm and along a rough lane. Just before the lane rises, fork left into woodland and alongside the River Wey through Tilford Nature Reserve, before the path veers right between houses to reach the northern side of The Green in Tilford.

Frensham Great Pond

Distance 8km **Time** 2 hours 15 **Terrain** waterside and woodland paths and lanes **Map** OS Explorer 145 **Access** bus to Frensham Great Pond from Farnham and Haslemere stops on the A287, 500m from the start (no Sunday service)

The larger of Frensham's ponds is the focus of a varied circuit with long views from the higher ground on the return.

The walk starts from Frensham Great Pond, where there is a large car park, a small café, a picnic area and toilets. It is an increasingly popular place, in particular at weekends and during the summer when the car park can quickly become full, though people have been coming here in large numbers since at least Victorian times to escape life in the city and for the open spaces of Frensham Common. A pond is recorded as having been in existence here as early as the start of the 13th century, when it belonged to the Bishop of Winchester and was stocked with fish for Farnham Castle, but the history of human occupation of the site goes back thousands of years before that. Today there is an angling society, sailing club and a beach with an area marked out for swimming.

From the bottom of the parking area, go right onto the path along the west side of the pond to Bacon Lane. Turn left and, halfway round the bend before Frensham Pond Hotel, turn right onto a bridleway for the next 1.3km. This leads into woodland and alongside a stream and then the River Wey, past a footbridge and the back of Frensham Manor to Mill Lane.

A left turn over the mill races and past the pond takes you to a junction with Pitt Lane. Turn left for just over 100m and then by Mill Cottage take the bridleway off right for the next 1km. This shortly curves left between fields and makes its way gently up to Bealeswood Lane and the houses of Dockenfield. Bear right along the lane which soon becomes a

FRENSHAM GREAT POND

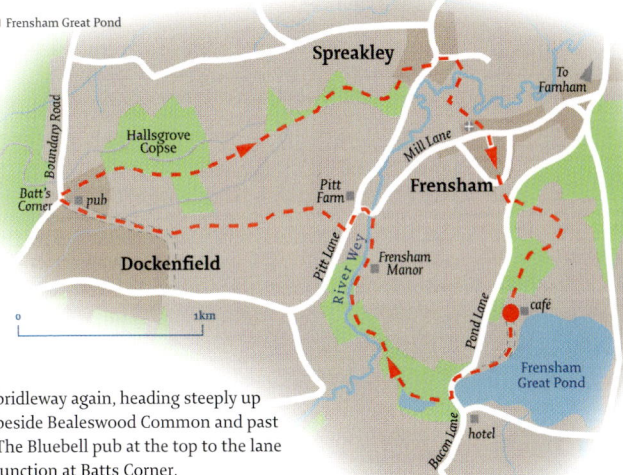

◀ Frensham Great Pond

bridleway again, heading steeply up beside Bealeswood Common and past The Bluebell pub at the top to the lane junction at Batts Corner.

Turn right onto Boundary Road, then immediately right again onto a footpath which heads along a driveway and passes to the right of a house to reach a stile into Hallsgrove Copse. At the far end of the woodland follow the right-hand field edge along the broad crest, with views over the Surrey Hills, and then down through a second copse. At the far end, the footpath passes along the edge of the next field and over a staggered crosspaths to a stile. This takes you back into woodland again for just over 100m, before heading along the right-hand field-edge and bending left. As you drop downhill, look out as the footpath turns sharp right along the backs of houses and then down a lane to emerge at the houses of Spreakley.

Walk across Pitt Lane and along Hammondswood Road for 100m to a crosspaths. A right turn downhill takes you across the River Wey and then alongside it, before the footpath bends left to Frensham Church. At the road dogleg left for 30m, then right along Lovers Lane, which soon becomes a footpath between houses. Cross over the estate road and continue between fields up to Bacon Lane. Another dogleg left, then right keeps you on the footpath which climbs up over the rise through woodland, with plenty of marker posts to show you the way, before descending to a bridleway junction. A right turn will take you back down to Frensham Great Pond.

Churt and Whitmoor Vale

Distance 6km **Time** 1 hour 45
Terrain lanes, bridleways and woodland
Map OS Explorer OL33 **Access** bus to Churt from Farnham and Hindhead

An undulating route ushers you up the old way through Whitmoor Vale and past now silent mills.

The walk starts from the centre of the village of Churt by The Crossways Inn. Churt lies close to the county boundary and has two streams which feed Frensham Ponds. The one to the north of the village flows down from the high ground around Hindhead, while to the south lies Whitmoor Vale. The stream here was used to drive two papermills and a cornmill from as long ago as the 13th century. Barford Mill is the middle of the three and was still grinding corn in the early 1900s. Parts of this mill date from the 14th century and inside is an old ship's mast around which the staircase is constructed. The old route from London passed through Whitmoor Vale and there is a room in the mill which served as a cell for those condemned to be transported on their way to take ship at Portsmouth.

Head up Churt Road, the A287, for 300m, along the pavement and then a grass verge, to the southern end of the village. A right turn down Kitts Lane takes you past Kitts Farm, with an old well in its front courtyard, and steeply down to the bottom of the vale. Bear left onto the bridleway to Barford Mill. Beyond, the bridleway rises gently up the side of Whitmoor Vale on a tree-lined track, with intermittent views across the valley. After just over 1km, it emerges at the junction with Whitmoor Vale Road.

Bear right along the road to continue ahead for 250m and take the second footpath on the left. This path heads

◂ One of the former mills in Whitmoor Vale

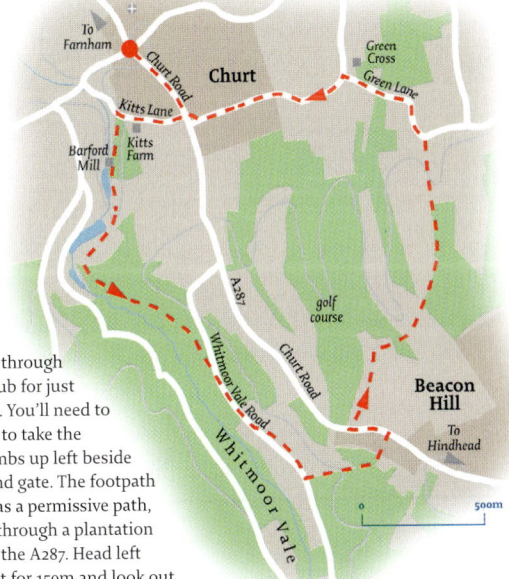

parallel to the road through trees and heath scrub for just over 250m to a gate. You'll need to brace yourself here to take the footpath which climbs up left beside the fence to a second gate. The footpath continues beyond as a permissive path, still steeply uphill through a plantation and then left up to the A287. Head left along the pavement for 150m and look out for a footpath sign off right.

The footpath, marked by posts, heads across Hindhead Golf Course along a track, passing some tall Scots pines before reaching a junction with a tarmac path after 250m. A short dogleg left, then right allows you to continue down past a marker post and across the steep-sided valley beyond. At the bottom you cross the fairway, so look out for golfers teeing off on the right.

On the far side of the valley, the footpath heads up into the trees before levelling out and bending to the left. You now pass through a plantation on a clear path and descend through some pleasant deciduous woodland to Green Lane. Here, turn left and follow the winding hands-in-pockets lane for just over 1km, bearing left at Green Cross House to descend to the southern end of Churt. Just before the A287 you can turn right down The Old Lane to return to the start.

Gibbet Hill and the Devil's Punch Bowl

Distance 10.5km **Time** 3 hours
Terrain lanes, byways and bridleways
Map OS Explorer OL33 **Access** bus from Hindhead and Haslemere stops on the A287 near Devil's Punch Bowl car park

Take the higher ground for a Surrey Hills classic from the village idyll of Thursley.

The walk starts from Thursley. Surrey's most famous architect, Edwin Lutyens spent part of his early life here at what is now Street House by The Clump, a grassy triangle with benches just down from The Three Horseshoes pub. He is perhaps as known in the county for his country-house designs, many in Arts and Crafts style, as his international commissions and his war memorials, notably the Cenotaph in Whitehall. Several Lutyens family graves are to be found in the churchyard of St Michael and All Angels.

Time looking round the church is well spent and there is an informative leaflet available. In the graveyard is the famous Sailor's Grave. This is the grave of an unnamed man who was murdered in 1786 on Hindheath Heath by three men whom he had met in a pub in the village. The three men were later convicted of the sailor's murder and hanged in Guildford. Their corpses were then hung in chains on what afterwards became known as Gibbet Hill and a little further on is a stone memorial to the incident.

From The Clump head along The Street past houses and turn right into Highfield Lane, walking up past the church for just over 1km to the top of the lane. Continue ahead onto the byway, which carries the Greensand Way, climbing steadily uphill for the next 2.5km. This takes you up a holloway, over a byway crossroads, signed for Gibbet Hill, then up through heath scrub and woodland and past where a bridleway joins from the left. Beyond this, continue uphill with increasingly good

GIBBET HILL AND THE DEVIL'S PUNCH BOWL

◀ The Sailor's Stone overlooking the Devil's Punch Bowl

views right across the Punch Bowl. As the track curves right, it passes a restored turnpike milestone and you can detour left to the top of Gibbet Hill with its triangulation pillar and Celtic Cross.

The byway now levels out and around the sweeping right bend passes the Sailor Stone memorial. Here, you are also passing above the Hindhead Tunnels through which the modern A3 now passes, but until 2011 the road passed over the top of the hill. Continue from the memorial for 400m to a bridleway junction and turn right over the line of the 1822 coach road, which later became the A3, to the main viewpoint over the Devil's Punch Bowl 300m beyond. You'll find a picnic area and National Trust café by the car park here.

The onward route continues along the bridleway, signed for Highcombe, into woodland and down to a gate into the National Trust area of Highcombe Edge. Keep along the broad crest with good views and after 400m, at a fork in the bridleway, keep right, passing a memorial to the Robertson brothers whose bequest enabled the National Trust to purchase the land hereabouts. After another 800m, you reach a bridleway crosspaths.

The route heads straight over and soon descends through a gate and more steeply down a holloway to reach Hyde Lane at a bend. Here, turn right up the narrow lane past Ridgeway Farm house, beyond which the lane becomes a byway and soon descends steeply to a footbridge across a brook. Climb steeply up the far side past cottages to the top of Highfield Lane. Turn left here and retrace your steps back down to Thursley.

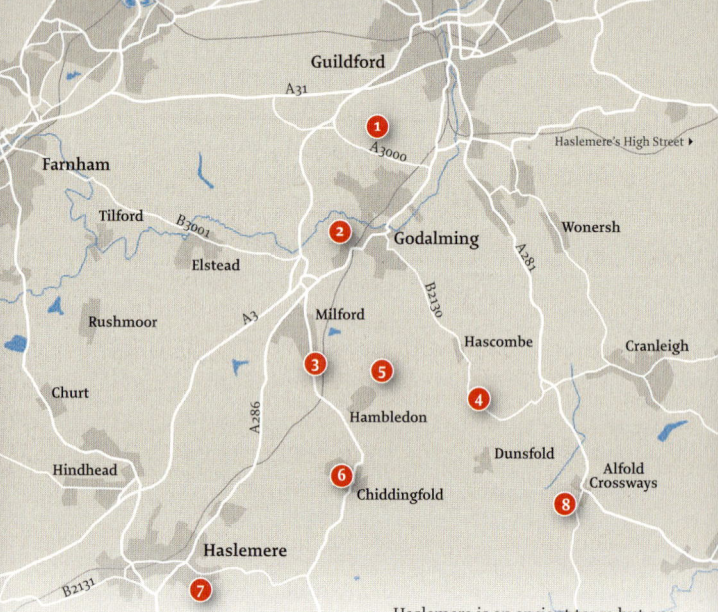

Haslemere's High Street ▶

This section is dominated by the two commuter towns of Godalming and Haslemere. When the boundary of the Surrey Hills AONB was initially drawn up, a significant portion of the countryside around Godalming, and to a lesser extent around Haslemere, was not included within its borders. This has to some extent been rectified by the creation and subsequent designation of Areas of Great Landscape Value. Nevertheless, since 1958 there have been repeated calls by campaigners to review the boundary. Such a review is currently underway and it is likely that much of this area will be brought within the protection of the AONB boundary.

Haslemere is an ancient town but one that saw a significant expansion in population and prosperity with the coming of the railways in the 19th century and the opening of the London to Portsmouth line. It also became a centre for the Arts and Crafts movement and this has added considerably to the architectural appeal of the town. It is the southernmost town in Surrey and sits close to the county borders with Hampshire and Sussex. It is also well-placed for walking, situated as it is right on the border between the southern limit of the Surrey Hills AONB and of the South Downs National Park, whose northern edge is dominated by the high ground of Black Down.

Godalming and Haslemere

1 Compton and the Artists' Village 28
Explore the fascinating Watts Gallery Artists' Village before looping back through parkland and woodland

2 Godalming and Eashing 30
Weave your way past remnants of the area's cloth industry on this riverside and woodland ramble

3 Witley 32
Take in some fine views of the Surrey Hills on this short loop from an historic village

4 Hascombe Hill 34
Don't miss the stunning interior of St Peter's Church before making the steep hike up the hill

5 Hambledon and Hydon's Ball 36
Visit a memorial to one of the founders of the National Trust on this rolling countryside walk

6 Chiddingfold 38
Stroll around a charming village with a glass-making history before touring surrounding woodland and bridleways

7 Haslemere and Black Down 40
Tennyson found daily inspiration at the viewpoint reached on this high-level circuit

8 Alfold and Sidney Wood 42
Discover sites of long-lost industry on this woodland walk from a charming village on the Surrey/Sussex border

Compton and the Artists' Village

Distance 7.5km **Time** 2 hours
Terrain lanes, woodland and fields
Map OS Explorer 145 **Access** bus to Compton from Godalming and Guildford

There is plenty to see and admire along this route, including the famous Watts Gallery Artists' Village and the parkland of Loseley House.

The walk starts from Compton, where there is some roadside parking on The Street, the B3000, running through the village or along Spiceall, the road running alongside the recreation ground on the north side of the B3000. Alternative starts are possible from The Withies Inn, which has roadside parking spaces opposite and its own car park, to the east of the village along Withies Lane by the side of Compton Common.

The fascinating Watts Gallery Artists' Village is situated a little way along the route of the walk on Down Lane. It too has parking available, if the intention likewise is to visit.

With the B3000 behind you at the junction with Spiceall, bear right over the recreation ground. On the far side, turn left up Polsted Lane for 400m, past Almsgate, and take the footpath off left just before Withies Lane. (If coming from The Withies Inn walk up to this junction and the footpath is opposite, a little to the left.) The footpath heads through Bummoor Copse and then alongside a paddock before doglegging right, then left up to a footpath and track junction. Turn left and follow the footpath along the track up to and then to the right of Coneycroft Farm to reach Down Lane, opposite the entrance to Limnerslease House and car park.

Limnerslease was home to George Frederic Watts, best known for his portraits, allegorical paintings and sculptures, and Mary Watts, his second

COMPTON AND THE ARTISTS' VILLAGE

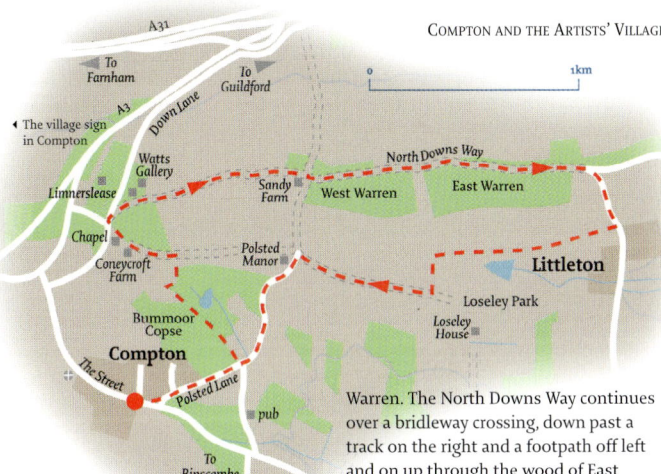

wife, who was also a renowned designer, potter and artist, and founded the Compton Pottery which eventually closed in the 1950s. The house was designed by the architect Sir Earnest George in 1891 and is open to the public.

The memorial chapel on Down Lane, designed and built by Mary, was completed in 1904, the year of her husband's death. Nearby, the Watts Gallery, designed by Sir Christoper Hatton Turnor, houses many of the Watts' works. Another gallery above the visitor centre and shop displays and sells works of contemporary artists and makers.

The route bears right in front of the Watts Gallery onto the North Downs Way and follows the broad sandy track for a little over 2km up over a rise and down past the buildings of Sandy Farm before heading up through the wood of West Warren. The North Downs Way continues over a bridleway crossing, down past a track on the right and a footpath off left and on up through the wood of East Warren to Littleton Lane.

Leave the North Downs Way here and turn right down the narrow lane for 350m to the crosspaths in the village of Littleton. Take the footpath which heads off right along a track between houses and over two fields to reach the lake of Loseley House, where the main house is visible over the parkland beyond. Once past the lake the route continues for another 200m between the fields, over a track and a little way along the edge of the next field before turning left up to a track.

A right turn takes you for just over 600m along this pleasant avenue lined with chestnut and lime trees past Polsted Lodge to houses at the top of Polsted Lane. Here, turn left past Polsted Manor and follow the meandering lane for 600m to Withies Lane, where you can turn left for the inn, right for Watts Gallery Artists' Village, or keep straight on to return to the village centre.

29

Godalming and Eashing

Distance 6.5km **Time** 1 hour 45
Terrain lanes, woodland and riverside paths, sections can be muddy
Map OS Explorer 145 **Access** bus to Godalming from Farnham, Guildford and Haslemere; trains to Godalming from Guildford and Haslemere

Eashing is famous for its surviving medieval bridges and Godalming is popular for its old townscape and long history. This walk combines both.

The walk starts from Godalming railway station. If arriving by car there is parking at the station, in town car parks or on Borough Road near the end of the route.

Godalming, along with Farnham and Guildford, used to be known for its cloth industry and in medieval times the production of woollen cloth had been introduced by the monks of Waverley Abbey. The River Wey provided the required power and resources for the watermills and the fulling process. At Eashing, upstream of Godalming, the double bridge over the River Wey built by the monks not only survives but still carries traffic. Near the bridge is Abbey Mill, now a business centre but formerly a corn and papermill under the control of Waverley Abbey.

Head down through the station's lower car park and turn left onto Westbrook Road, under the railway and immediately left up New Way, which carries a bridleway and the Fox Way past the rear of the station. (If arriving by train you can exit the back of the station and turn left onto New Way.) After another 250m, New Way bears right and becomes a narrow lane rising through trees. At the top of the hill, keep ahead with the bridleway along New Way as it twists its way right and then back left past the housing development of

GODALMING AND EASHING

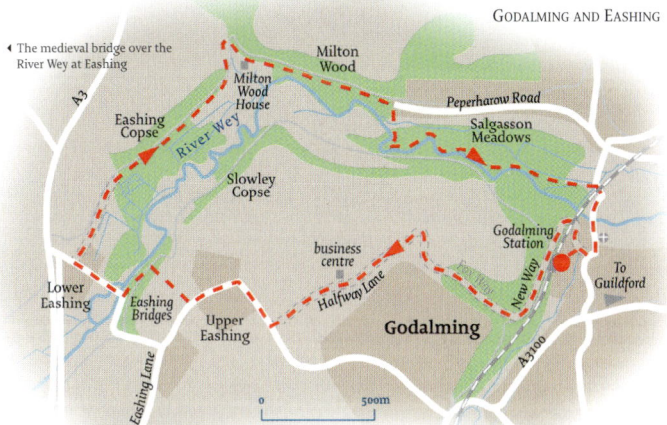

◀ The medieval bridge over the River Wey at Eashing

Ockford Park estate on the left. Continue past a small business centre on the right and along Halfway Lane to the junction with Eashing Lane.

Turn right along the pavement and then use the grass verges to make your way round the left bend in Upper Eashing. Continue along the road for another 200m, where a little care is needed with any traffic, and take the footpath off right with the Fox Way, which heads down the right-hand field edge and then bends to the left down through woodland and alongside the River Wey to Eashing Bridges. A little further along the road you will find the former site of Abbey Mill.

Head over the medieval double bridge and in 200m, just before the A3, turn right onto a bridleway down the lane past Greenways Stables and along a concrete track for 300m to a gate, where the track bends left. The bridleway continues ahead alongside Eashing Copse for 700m, with the River Wey off to the right across water meadows, before bending left up to a crosspaths.

Here, turn right onto the footpath and along the driveway to Milton Wood house. You now fork left onto a narrower footpath along the bottom of the slope of Milton Wood and then the edge of the water meadows, where there are sections of boardwalk, to reach the houses at the end of Peperharow Road.

Turn right down to the River Wey, where a left turn takes you onto the pleasant winding riverside path beside Salgasson Meadows and then alongside a stream on the left to bring you to Borough Road. Turn right along the pavement, under the railway and over the River Wey, beyond which Vicarage Walk off right will take you back towards the station, or you can head left by Phillips Memorial Park, which commemorates the chief wireless telegraphist on the *Titanic*, up past the parish church to explore the town centre.

Witley

Distance 3.5km **Time** 1 hour
Terrain lanes, woodland and fields
Map OS Explorer OL33 **Access** bus to Witley from Godalming and Haslemere

This short but satisfying walk up to the edge of Witley Common offers good views over the Surrey Hills.

The walk starts from the southern edge of the village of Witley at the junction of the A283 with Church Lane. There is some parking available near the bottom of Church Lane and opposite at the White Hart Inn, if the intention is to visit, or at the small parking area 150m up Church Lane past the school.

The White Hart lays claim to be one of the oldest sites for an inn in the country and a hostelry has stood here alongside the road, now the busy A283, since at least the days in June 1305 when Edward I held court here, though the oldest parts of the current establishment date from Elizabethan times. More recently, Witley provided a retreat for artists and writers, not least George Eliot, who bought a house here on the proceeds of her novel *Daniel Deronda*. A little up from the junction of Church Lane towards the village centre is George Eliot Close.

Head up Church Lane for 150m, passing the church and the school. Turn right onto the footpath through the small parking area and pass to the right of Witley Lodge along a hedged path parallel with a lane and houses on the right. The path soon descends through woodland and bends left to a flight of steps. Head down the steps and round a garden with an ornamental lake to a footpath junction by the entrance to Lower Roke House. Cross the driveway and keep ahead up through woodland to a second path junction at the top edge of the wood.

◀ Ornamental lake by Lower Roke House

Continue ahead uphill out of the trees up a track past some cottages on the southern edge of Witley Common. By the last one, Mare House, fork left into the trees and soon join a track which descends to Mare Hill Cottage.

The route now heads into fields along a fenced path for 250m up to a gate, where the path splits. The left fork takes you up the shoulder of the hill, with increasingly good views back over the Surrey Hills around Godalming and Guildford. Just before reaching Winkford Farm there is currently a footpath diversion which circles round to the left of the house and garden to reach the driveway on the far side, where a left turn takes you down to Church Lane.

Turn left down the narrow lane and after 300m you can continue downhill on the path on the right, above and parallel to the deeply sunken road, with a good view across the valley between the trees for the final part back down past the parking area to Witley.

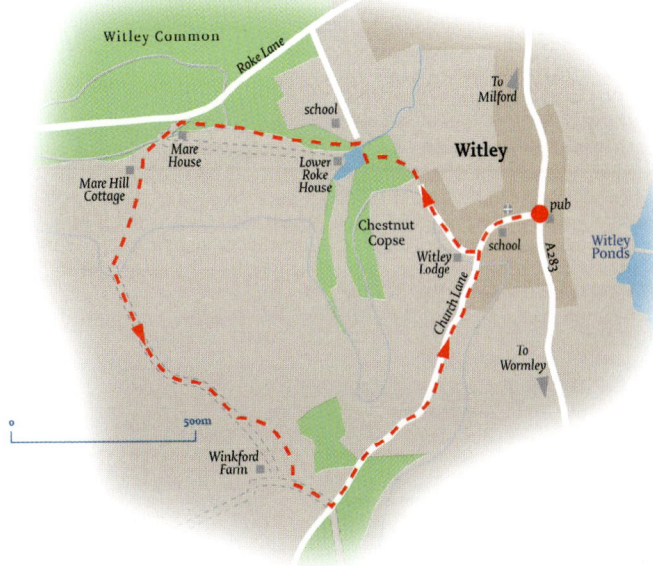

Hascombe Hill

Distance 3.5km **Time** 1 hour 15
Terrain lanes and woods, with a sustained climb **Map** OS Explorer OL34
Access bus to Hascombe from Godalming

A short route with a steep start gives access to a wooded hillfort and an unusual church nearby.

The walk starts on the southern edge of the village of Hascombe, at the junction of the B2130 with Church Road and Nore Lane, where there is a parking area off the B2130, opposite The White Horse pub.

Before or after the walk it is worth taking a stroll along Church Road to see the large village pond surrounded by cottages and St Peter's Church. The current church was built in the 1860s and replaced a far older building, though the style in general is of the 13th century. It has strong connections with the Oxford Movement and Sir John Betjeman called it a 'Tractarian work of art'. Inside you are in for a surprise as the walls, windows and roof are highly decorated. Vernon Musgrave, rector in the second half of the 19th century, commissioned a group of freelance painters to execute the paintings. Of particular note is the painting of the 153 fish surrounding St Peter the fisherman and the Last Judgement on the chancel arch.

Head past the White Horse pub up Nore Lane, which carries a bridleway, and in 100m, just past Hascombe Place Farmhouse, take the footpath off right over a stile into woodland and up a holloway. In 150m, at the fork, bear left fairly steeply uphill for 300m and, as the gradient eases, keep an eye out for a marker post at the next fork. This time bear right and follow the narrower path as it contours and climbs with intermittent

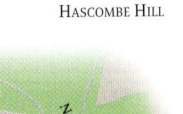

views across the valley to meet a path junction in front of the earthworks of the fort on top of Hascombe Hill. The fort is pre-Roman and has been dated to about 100BC. There is some evidence to suggest that it was destroyed by fire.

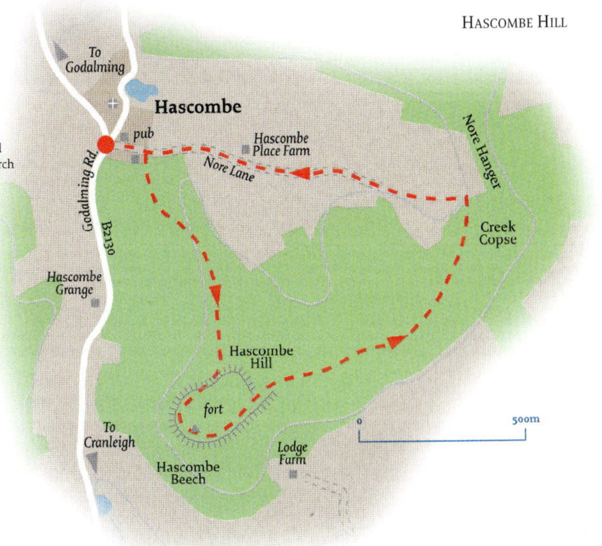

Turn right and follow the path beside the earthworks around to the left and onto the southern end of the hill. Once on the southern side it's possible to scramble up and explore the area of the fort, though it is mostly covered in trees and shrubs, of which there is a good variety, including beech, laurel, chestnut, rhododendron, pine, sycamore, silver birch, spruce, holly, rowan, and oak.

At the end of the prominent earthworks continue along the southern edge of the hill in an ENE direction for another 350m, past a track on the left, to a fork in the path. Keep a look-out for the footpath marker disc, currently on a silver birch tree in the middle of the fork – if you miss the fork, you will find yourself descending a forestry track which zigzags down the hill's southern slope. At the fork the footpath branches left and climbs slightly for another 200m over the rise. You now start the descent and pass through an old metal fence, before heading down through Creek Copse, with the steep ground now on your left, to a junction with a bridleway at the bottom below Nore Hanger.

Here, a left turn brings you out of the trees and it's a simple task to follow the bridleway downhill, with a good view down the valley, past the buildings of Hascombe Place Farm and along Nore Lane to the start.

Hambledon and Hydon's Ball

Distance 6.5km **Time** 1 hour 45
Terrain lanes, fields and woods; a climb up Hydon's Ball **Map** OS Explorer OL33
Access bus to Hambledon village centre from Godalming

The memorial to a National Trust founder is the first objective on a walk that loops around fields and woodland into the hidden folds of Buss's Common.

The walk starts from St Peter's Church in Hambledon, situated at the north end of the village along Church Lane. There is a small parking area at the lane end and some roadside space by the church.

Take the footpath alongside the graveyard wall past an old limekiln into fields, across the first field, then diagonally left across the second to Fourteen Acre Copse. Once through the gate into the woodland, the path veers to the right past a clearing and through trees up to a crosspaths. Turn left for 250m uphill and round to the right to a fork in the path. Keep left with the footpath past a memorial to W A Robertson, who purchased the land around Hydon's Ball for the National Trust, and just beyond you can make a short detour off right up to the top of Hydon's Ball and its triangulation pillar for good views over the South Downs.

You will also find a granite seat here, a memorial to Octavia Hill, one of the three founding members of the National Trust. She was a social reformer, supported by John Ruskin amongst others, and did much to improve the conditions of people living in poor areas of London.

Continue along the footpath beside a chainlink fence and descend past a house and garden to a crosspaths. A left turn takes you along a bridleway, down out of the wood and then between fields to Hambledon Road. The bridleway carries on across the road along a track for 400m

and soon passes through West Surrey golf course to the cottages at Potter's Barn. Beyond, follow the bridleway across two fairways – look out for flying golf balls here – and on the far side of the second fairway turn left onto a footpath.

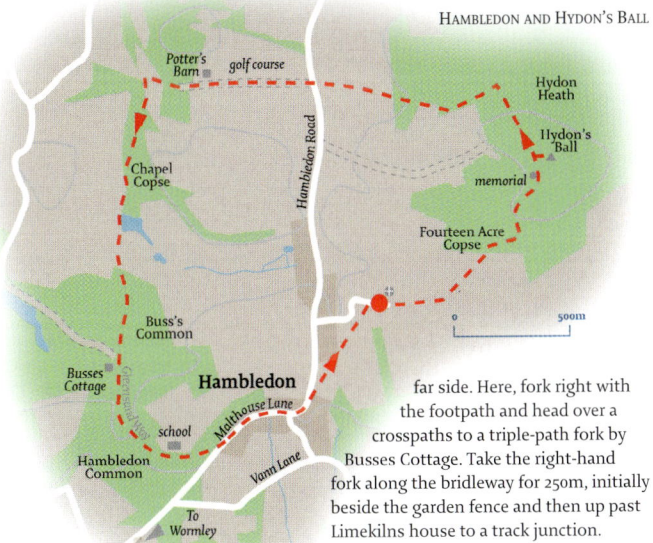

This footpath heads up the right-hand edge of the fairway for 100m before veering right at a marker post into woodland and descending to a footbridge. Dogleg right across the bridge then left to keep on the footpath which soon heads up out of the trees and bears left along the edge of a field and past a small lake to a gate into wooded Buss's Common.

In 50m, by the end of the electricity lines, fork left with the footpath which heads through the mixed woodland and across a clearing towards the trees on the far side. Here, fork right with the footpath and head over a crosspaths to a triple-path fork by Busses Cottage. Take the right-hand fork along the bridleway for 250m, initially beside the garden fence and then up past Limekilns house to a track junction.

Across the track take the left-hand of two bridleways past Moor Cottage, uphill on the route of the Greensand Way. Near the top of the rise, fork left off the bridleway to keep on the Greensand Way onto a footpath up past a topograph and views to the South Downs, before continuing to contour to the left round Hambledon Common and descending down to Malthouse Lane. Turn left along this lane past Malthouse Farm and through the village to the junction with Woodlands Road. Continue round the bend – a bit of care is needed here – and once past Hemingway House take the footpath off right, rising steeply uphill. You'll need a bit of puff for this final climb up to a gate and across the two fields beyond, with the tower of St Peter's Church to guide you back to the start.

◀ Looking back over fields near Fourteen Acre Copse

ary's Church, follow Mill Lane for
Chiddingfold

Distance 8km **Time** 2 hours
Terrain lanes, woods and fields
Map OS Explorer OL33 **Access** bus to
Chiddingfold from Guildford, Godalming
and Haslemere

A varied walk with some fine views begins from one of Surrey's most picturesque villages.

The walk starts from the centre of the village of Chiddingfold, where there is parking by The Green. The Crown Inn by its bottom corner is well known, and near it is the more than 500-year-old hawthorn tree, still growing between Thorn Cottage and Forrest Stores. Opposite is the Old Forge, a reminder that the centre of Chiddingfold was once busier than today's grassy expanse surrounded by attractive cottages and houses suggests. Glass-making was once a thriving industry in the village. Ready sources of charcoal, limestone and sand here and elsewhere in southwest Surrey meant that in the 16th century there were eleven glassworks around The Green, supplying glass for churches and buildings in London and other cities.

From The Green, walk down past The Crown Inn and, across the A283 below St Mary's Church, follow Mill Lane for 1km past houses and cottages and the entrance to Sydenhurst. Beyond this, the lane continues uphill past the entrance to Sydenhurst Farm. Continue ahead onto the bridleway along the driveway to Hollyhurst and, in front of its entrance, fork left to stay on the bridleway through woodland on a wide path to West End Lane. A left turn along this lane takes you past Furzefield house and down past Dell Farm in a dip. Just beyond, fork right, signed for Frillinghurst, onto a bridleway that leads up the lane to Frillinghurst Old Manor at the top.

Keep right of the modern house here and follow the bridleway into Frillinghurst Wood and over a staggered

◀ The village pond in Chiddingfold Copse

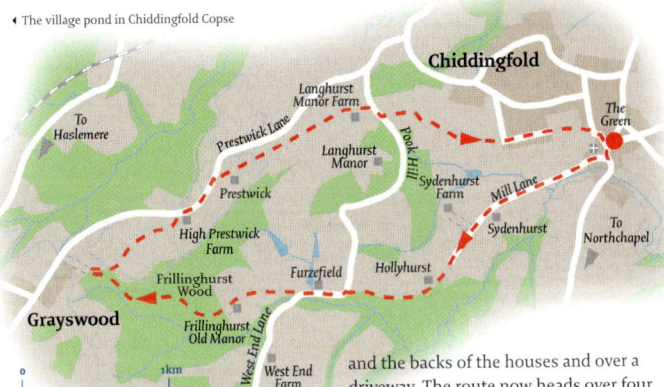

crosspaths to reach a triple-path fork a little over 100m further on. Take the middle path to stay on the bridleway, now narrower, which twists its way for 350m to meet a track coming in from the left, before heading up to a clearing, where a track joins on the right. Keep ahead on the now broad, meandering track for the next 500m to a crosspaths between two unusual square yellow pipe-arches.

A sharp right turn through a gate leads you into fields onto a footpath along the right-hand edge of the first field before a left turn up the second takes you through double gates at the top of the rise with good views back to the south over Black Down and towards Haslemere. The path now descends along field edges and through a copse to reach Prestwick Lane.

Turn right along the lane through the hamlet of Prestwick for 300m to Prestwick Cottage, where a footpath heads off right. Follow the waymarks across two gardens and the backs of the houses and over a driveway. The route now heads over four fields before crossing over a footpath in a wooded hollowway and over a fifth field to reach a footpath junction by woodland. Keep ahead through the woodland to the lane at Pook Hill.

A dogleg right up the lane, over the brow past Langhurst Manor for 50m, then left takes you onto a footpath over fields again. At the end of the first field you'll need to zigzag along a fenced section between two Lutyens-designed houses into a second field. Follow the footpath over the rise and then a crosspaths and along the left-hand field edge to a stile at the far end. Keep ahead along the backs of gardens to a lane which now takes you past the fronts of houses. At the end of the lane a footpath continues ahead into trees and descends down past the graveyard of St Mary's Church. Here, you can turn right through the graveyard to visit the church, or continue on a little way to Coxcombe Lane and turn right, to return to the centre of Chiddingfold.

Haslemere and Black Down

Distance 12km **Time** 3 hours 30
Terrain lanes, fields and open heathland, with a cumulative climb of 300m
Map OS Explorer OL33 **Access** bus to Haslemere from Farnham and Guildford; trains to Haslemere from Guildford

This higher-level walk takes you over the county border from the southern edge of the Surrey Hills to the highest point in Sussex. Queen Victoria's Poet Laureate, Alfred Lord Tennyson, is said to have walked to the Temple of the Winds viewpoint from his home at nearby Aldworth House almost every day.

From the top of the High Street in the centre of Haslemere by the town hall and war memorial, head left in the direction of Petworth along the B2131 Petworth Road for 150m and turn left onto the footpath down Collards Lane into the National Trust-owned land of Swan Barn Farm. As the lane bends right, you join the Serpent Trail (Tail Route) whose waymarks are followed for the majority of the walk. The trail heads along to the end of the lane and then along the left-hand edge of two fields to a gate into woodland. You now turn right through Witley Copse, over a track and up the left-hand edge of the wood to reach Petworth Road again.

A short dogleg left, then right takes you onto a bridleway down Pine Springs Valley. This lane, initially tarmac, descends to gates to Lythehill Estate and then forks left down a rough lane and through woodland to cross a stream in a dip. You then climb to a gate at the top of the wood and up the field beyond to High Barn Farm. Continue along the driveway to a gate, where the Serpent Trail bends left and rises steadily between fields and alongside woodland, with views left over the Surrey Hills, up to Tennyson's Lane.

Here, turn right and follow the steep wooded lane uphill for the next 800m up to the sharp right-hand bend. Keep on round the bend for 200m to the main

HASLEMERE AND BLACK DOWN

◀ Heading west over Black Down

National Trust car park on Black Down. Here, the Serpent Trail turns left past the car park and then a triangulation pillar and information board. From here it's a simple task to follow the Serpent Trail waymarks for the next 1.5km over Black Down and through the woods to the viewpoint at the Temple of the Winds.

From the Temple of the Winds and its topograph pointing out the views over the South Downs, the Serpent Trail circles back sharp right (take care not to stray to the left downhill) and heads back over the western side of the top of Black Down on a clear path. After 700m you pass a topograph and some benches to take in the views westwards before descending to a bridleway junction with the Sussex Border Path.

The Serpent Trail now turns left to head northwestwards with the Sussex Border Path across the top of Black Down, down its western slopes and through light woodland before bending to the right and contouring northwards to a gate. The trail then leads down through Chase Wood and bends left to a gate into fields. Bear right across the first field and then sharp left down the edge of the second to a gate at the bottom. From here, the Serpent Trail descends to a lane and continues to the right down the lane past Valewood Farm House before bending left along a track to a stream by Stedlands Farm.

Here, you leave the Serpent Trail and turn right past Stedlands Farm. In another 50m make sure you fork left onto a byway into woodland which heads steeply uphill to Scotland Lane. A short dogleg left along the lane, then right takes you onto a fenced footpath for 500m between gardens and the recreation ground, over Hill Road and down steps to bring you out onto Petworth Road again. Turn left along the pavement to return to the centre of Haslemere.

Alfold and Sidney Wood

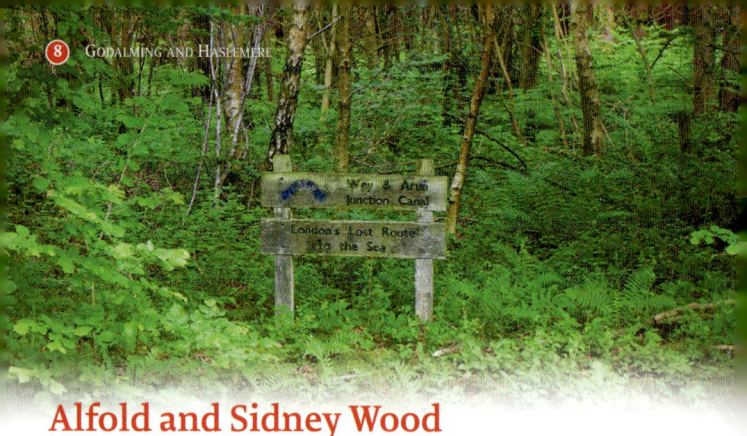

Distance 7km **Time** 1 hour 45
Terrain lanes, woodland and canal towpath **Map** OS Explorer OL34
Access bus to Alfold from Guildford, Godalming and Cranleigh

There's plenty of history on this route through woods once used for glassmaking and along London's 'Lost Route to the Sea'.

The walk starts from the village of Alfold, at the junction of the B2133 with Rosemary Lane near the Church of St Nicholas. There is some roadside parking at the end of Rosemary Lane or alongside the B2133. Alfold lies just north of the county border with Sussex, with Sidney Wood to its west. Here, in the mid-1960s the remains of glass-making furnaces were unearthed by archaeologists. Some of the remains dated to the 16th century, when several glassworkers from France came to work in the area. One of these was Jean le Carré, a Huguenot from Arras in the Artois region of northern France. He was known in England as John Carré, or John Tarry, and had learned his trade in Antwerp before fleeing to England to escape Catholic hostility during the French Wars of Religion. He applied new glass-making techniques here and in his London workshops that greatly improved the production of window glass, drinking glasses, glass bowls, plates and medical and distilling apparatus. He died in 1572 and is believed to be buried in the churchyard, near the war memorial, where a slab of marble marks the probable site of his grave.

Head up Rosemary Lane for 1km past cottages and the entrance to Turtles Farm and continue between fields to the southwest corner of Park Copse and the junction with the bridleway of Sachelhill Lane. The route now turns right into the woodland and heads northwards for just under 1km up Sachelhill Lane bridleway, gently climbing to a crosspaths and marker post. Turn left off the bridleway onto the waymarked footpath, which

ALFOLD AND SIDNEY WOOD

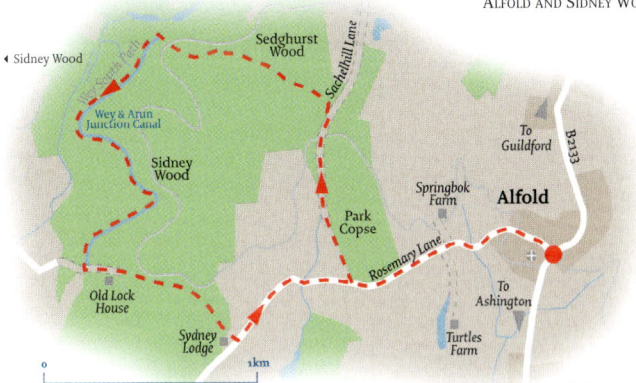

immediately doglegs right and then left through the mixed forestry of Sedghurst Wood. After 200m you cross over a track, and in another 150m you come to a path T-junction. Bear left and descend gently for 100m to a fork in the path, where you should bear right to reach a driveway a little way down from a house.

Cross over the driveway and turn left onto the bridleway and the route of the Wey South Path, which forks right after 50m and descends gently through the trees for 300m to meet the Wey and Arun Junction Canal. This is London's 'Lost Route to the Sea' and is being restored, with the aim to reach the sea at Arundel. The first section currently holds water, but it is unlikely that boats will once again pass along it on their way from the Thames to the English Channel. The canal was constructed in the early 1800s to link the Wey Navigation Channel in Surrey to the Arun Navigation Channel in Sussex. Barges imported groceries, coal, provisions and even seaweed for use as fertiliser, while carrying away timber, flour and farm produce. However, after just 50 years the railways provided cheaper and faster transport and the canal soon fell into disrepair.

Head over the canal, turn left and follow the towpath for the next 1.5km as it meanders its way south through Sidney Wood, passing a number of distance markers and a disused lock whose structure is still just visible. Beyond the lock you round a sweeping left-hand bend to arrive at Knightons Lane. A left turn along the lane, which carries a bridleway, takes you past the entrance to Old Lock House and through a metal barrier onto a track through the lower part of Sidney Wood. Keep ahead on the broad bridleway for 600m, ignoring paths and tracks off left and right, to Sydney Lodge by Rosemary Lane at the southeastern corner of the wood. Now turn left and follow the lane for 700m as it twists and turns its way to the junction with Sachellhill Lane, from where you can retrace steps for the final 1km back to Alfold.

Guildford is often thought of as the county town of Surrey. However, this lies to the north at Kingston upon Thames, now part of Greater London, while Reigate has become the main administrative centre. The countryside to the east and southeast of Guildford comprises the heart of the Surrey Hills. The areas to the northeast around West Horsley and in the far south beyond Cranleigh currently lie just outside the AONB boundary, but this is likely to change with the current review.

The villages of Shalford, Chilworth, Albury, Shere and Gomshall, which lie along the A248 and A25, are some of the prettiest in the whole county. For this reason, they have become even more popular for every type of visitor, drawn by the rows of wooden-framed and tile-hung cottages, cafés and tearooms, churches and greens and village halls, all surrounded by woods and fields. However, their narrow lanes were never meant to carry the weight of modern traffic and their ever-growing popularity is now requiring careful management, including an encouragement to use the railway for access and the creation of new cycle lanes.

To the south, the land towards Cranleigh becomes wooded and rises to the high ground of Hurtwood Common, culminating in the highest point in this part of the Surrey Hills at Pitch Hill on top of the Greensand Ridge above Peaslake and Holmbury St Mary. Below, the ground drops away towards Ewhurst and Cranleigh, with long views on clear days to the Low Weald of West Sussex and the South Downs beyond.

Fields between Chilworth and St Martha's Hill looking west ▶

Guildford

1 West Horsley and Sheepleas 46
Take in an ancient semi-natural woodland with wildflowers growing on the chalk downs

2 Chilworth and St Martha's Hill 48
Make the pilgrimage from Surrey's former gunpowder centre to visit a hill with a grim history

3 Wonersh and Chinthurst Hill 50
Hike up a steep-sided hill through mixed woodland to enjoy a Caledonian folly and wonderful views

4 Shere and Newlands Corner 52
One of Surrey's prettiest villages is the start point for this climb up chalk grassland slopes to a high viewpoint

5 Peaslake and Pitch Hill 54
Join mountain bikers and trailrunners enjoying access to this vast area of woodland and common

6 Holmbury Hill 56
Bask in extensive views from one of Surrey's best-known and most popular high points

7 Ewhurst 58
Cross the old road to Londinium and explore the traces of Roman life on this easy circuit

8 Walliswood 60
Follow the lanes to a quiet and secluded woodland alive with butterflies and flowers

West Horsley and Sheepleas

Distance 6km **Time** 1 hour 30
Terrain lanes, fields and woodland
Map OS Explorer 145 **Access** bus to West Horsley from Guildford and Leatherhead

An enchanting varied route guides you over parkland, through a nature reserve and back along a hidden dell.

The walk begins at the southern end of West Horsley village. Start at the crossroads of Ripley Lane and Cranmore Lane by the village orchard, 400m up The Street from the A246 Epsom Road. Parking is possible along The Street or on Cranmore Lane. The route passes through the Sheepleas, an area of ancient semi-natural woodland and grassland with an abundance of wildflowers on the chalk slopes of the downs. As the name suggests, the original use of the land was for grazing, but now it is a reserve managed by Surrey Wildlife Trust. There has been woodland here for at least 400 years, and since the devastating effects of the great storm in 1987 there has been a move to replace non-native species with those found naturally occurring on the downs, such as beech, maple, cherry, ash, whitebeam and yew.

Head up Cranmore Lane and round the left bend, continuing along the bridleway past the school playing field to the bend. Here, take the footpath ahead along the field edge beside Cranmore Wood and then bear right into a large second field and take the footpath alongside the fence. This leads you in 500m up to the A246 opposite St Mary's Church.

Across the road follow the bridleway past the church for 100m up to and through the main car park. The bridleway continues out the far end of the car park through woodland up onto Sheepleas. The wide path soon starts to climb and

WEST HORSLEY AND SHEEPLEAS

◀ Summer flowers near Hillside Farm

then curves right up to a picnic area and clearing at Angel Clump. Continue down the far side to a bridleway crosspaths and turn left uphill for 150m before forking right with the bridleway through the trees to a T-junction. Bear right, with a field on the left, to the driveway to Hillside Manor.

The route goes left here, climbing uphill on a fenced bridleway which curves its way up the slope to bring you to the west of Hillside Manor. There is a good view back to the north here before you turn right along its driveway to Shere Road. Turn right down the narrow road round the bend and take the bridleway off to the left up the entrance track to Hillside Farm. The track zigzags its way up past some stables and along a tree-lined track for 150m to the bend.

Here, turn right onto a fenced footpath, which heads alongside a field and then to the right down steps into Daws Dene.

This section is prone to being a little overgrown, so a stick may come in handy. The footpath heads down this delightful hidden valley with a long view northwards and then continues down along a narrow hedged and fenced section to bring you out onto a driveway by Chalk Pit Cottages after 500m. Turn right to emerge onto Shere Road, where a left turn takes you down over the A246 and back into West Horsley.

Chilworth and St Martha's Hill

Distance 8.5km **Time** 2 hours 30
Terrain woodland tracks and field paths
Map OS Explorer 145 **Access** bus and train to Chilworth from Guildford and Dorking

Follow a now tranquil route past bygone gunpowder mills and along the highway formerly trodden by pilgrims.

The walk starts from the eastern end of the long village of Chilworth by the railway station, where there is roadside parking on Dorking Road, the A248. Walk along the pavement past the school and turn right along Vera's Path. This footpath follows the line of a former tramway, past an information board on Chilworth Gunpowder Mills and over New Cut channel to a picnic area in the Middle Works of the site of the former gunpowder mills. Turn left along the heritage trail, where marker posts help you identify the parts of the former gunpowder mills, to the gate at West Lodge. Explosions at the works were a constant threat and they occurred with fateful regularity since the first powder mills were established here by the East India Company in the 1620s. One explosion, in 1763, even brought down the tower of St Martha's Church on the hill above the village, and the 'Great Explosion' of 1901 at the Black Conning House killed six workers, before the last powder mill closed in 1922.

At West Lodge, a right turn along Blacksmith Lane to the bend takes you past another former gunpowder mill and, just before the Tilling Bourne, the building which used to house the publishers Unwins. At the bend, a footpath forks off left up between gardens and along a left-hand field-edge with a good view right to St Martha's Hill, before passing the backs of more gardens to reach Halfpenny Lane.

Turn left onto the bridleway

CHILWORTH AND ST MARTHA'S HILL

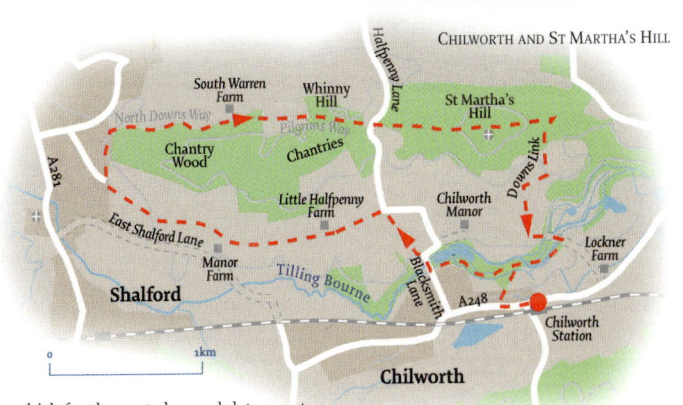

which for the next 1km undulates west along field edges towards Shalford, down past the barns of Little Halfpenny Farm and up over the rise to the buildings of Manor Farm. Here, the route forks right onto a footpath to continue along the field edge for another 800m towards the houses on Clifford Manor Road. Turn right up the road for 30m to the bend and then fork right up a sunken footpath over the rise to the junction with the North Downs Way by Chantry Wood and car park.

The route now turns right and heads east along the North Downs Way, mainly uphill for the next 1.5km, along the shady track past South Warren Farm and between fields. It then leads through the eastern end of Chantry Wood to reach Halfpenny Lane again, both reminders that you are now on the Pilgrims Way, though no longer subject to the halfpenny toll. You need to make a short dogleg left, then right to stay on the North Downs Way for the steeper climb to the top of St Martha's Hill, with its church and topograph marking out the views. The church was rebuilt in the 1850s, having fallen into disrepair. The dedication to St Martha dates from the 13th century and medieval pilgrims must certainly have been awed by the story that the name was a corruption of 'martyr', and that the place, commonly called Martirhill, marked the spot where early Christians had been martyred by pagan Saxons.

From the top, head down the North Downs Way for 300m to a junction with a bridleway on the right. Continue ahead for another 100m to a crosspaths. Here, the onward route leaves the North Downs Way and turns sharp right onto the Downs Link bridleway, which winds its way downhill for 800m to the junction with the track to Lockner Farm. Turn left down the track for 200m and just over the Tilling Bourne turn right, off the Downs Link, through a gate into the Middle Works of the gunpowder mills once more. Follow the path through the trees past the remains of the Boiler House and fork right to reach the picnic area again, where a left turn back along Vera's Path will return you to the start.

◀ St Martha's Church

Wonersh and Chinthurst Hill

Distance 6km **Time** 1 hour 45
Terrain former railway track, lanes and fields, with a steep climb up Chinthurst Hill **Map** OS Explorer 145 **Access** bus to Wonersh from Guildford and Cranleigh

Enjoy a lovely village, an old railway line and long views from a Caledonian folly on top of a steep-sided hill.

The walk starts from the centre of Wonersh by The Grantley Arms and the Village Stores. Parking is possible on the roadside in the village.

Head along The Street, the B2128, towards Bramley along the pavement and through the bends past The Gatehouse, which gives access to The Green beyond. There is an information board which gives a detailed account of how this unusual Green, hidden as it is behind high walls, came into being after Wonersh Park, the former home of the Grantley family, was demolished in the 1930s. A local benefactor, Beatrice Cook, purchased The Green soon afterwards for 'the quiet use of the adult residents of the village'. Continue along the road, round the left-hand bend to head down Station Road and over the River Wey. Keep along the pavement past houses for another 300m to the former railway station of Bramley and Wonersh.

A right turn takes you onto the Wey South Path and Downs Link along the former railway line, which now also carries the National Route 22 cyclepath. This tree-lined track passes through the former station and then along the backs of houses and sports fields for 600m before doglegging to the right over the River Wey. Here, you leave the Wey South Path and fork right onto a footpath over the meadow to Tannery Lane. Bear right with the Downs Link bridleway, which rises parallel with the lane up past houses to the junction with Chinthurst Lane.

The Downs Link bridleway continues across the road and gently up between

WONERSH AND CHINTHURST HILL

◀ The folly on top of Chinthurst Hill

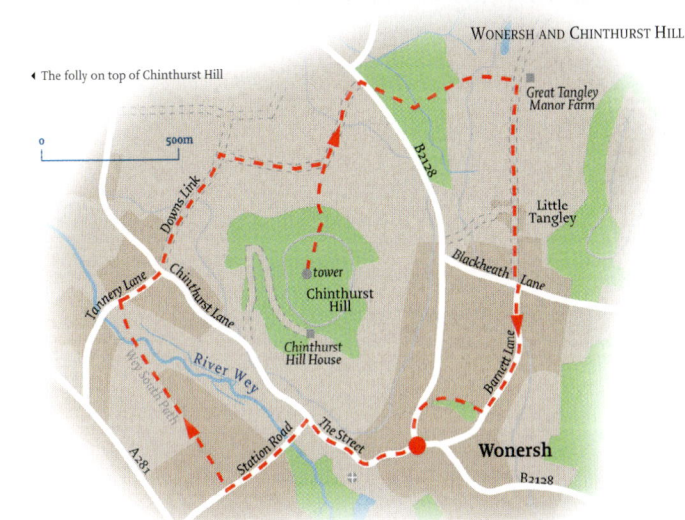

fields to the top of the rise before bending sharp right to reach a path T-junction on the north side of Chinthurst Hill after 400m. Turn right, signed for the Tower, and follow the waymarked trail steeply up through the woods for just under 500m to the tower on top of Chinthurst Hill, where a topograph marks out the view.

The tower ruin was built in the 1930s as a folly by Kenneth Mackay, 2nd Earl of Inchcape, echoing the architecture of his family seat, Glenapp Castle on the west coast of Scotland. The attractive pine trees on the summit were planted at the same time to complete the Caledonian diorama. A little further on is a well and on the south side of the hill is Mackay's former home, Chinthurst Hill House, an early commission of architect Edwin Lutyens, with formal gardens designed by Gertrude Jekyll.

Retrace steps to the T-junction at the base of the hill and carry on down the bridleway, which can be muddy, past the car park to the B2128. The Downs Link continues across the road on a narrow path that leads through the woodland to a lane after 200m. A left turn along the lane, which carries a bridleway, round the right-hand bend takes you up to a crosspaths by Great Tangley Manor.

Now turn right, off the Downs Link, and follow the footpath between fields to the houses of Little Tangley, where a short dogleg left, then right keeps you on the footpath towards the outskirts of Wonersh. At the houses on Blackheath Lane keep ahead along Barnett Lane for 500m and, where the houses on the right end, take the footpath off right past the playing field and cricket ground and then bear left to return to the centre of the village.

Shere and Newlands Corner

Distance 8.5km **Time** 2 hours 30 **Terrain** lanes, fields and tracks; a climb up to Newlands **Map** OS Explorer 145 **Access** bus to Shere from Guildford and Dorking

Saunter around one of Surrey's loveliest villages before heading for the high vantage point of Newlands Corner.

The walk starts from the village of Shere, where there is a free car park by the cricket field on London Lane just off Upper Street. On a summer's day there is perhaps no lovelier village in the Surrey Hills and people flock here, drawn by the houses and cottages dating from the 17th century or even earlier, the small shops, pubs, tearooms, and cafés. The Tilling Bourne flows through the village near the church, which is worth a visit to see the Millennium Stone in the churchyard beyond the lychgate designed by Edwin Lutyens. The church itself dates from the 12th century and inside there are memorials to the local Bray family, who donated the Millennium Stone. The church is also famed for its unusual hermit's cell, built in the 14th century for a local woman.

Head down Middle Street through the centre of the village and, on the far side of the Tilling Bourne, turn right along Lower Street past cottages and houses. At the ford, bear right over the stream and continue up Rectory Lane. After just over 100m, bear left onto a footpath which leads up between gardens, over Chantry Lane and up through light woodland to a gate into fields.

The path heads along the left-hand field edge, over the driveway to Albury Park and, in another 150m, forks left through a gate into Silver Wood and over a rise. At the far side of the wood continue over the

◀ On Middle Street in the village of Shere

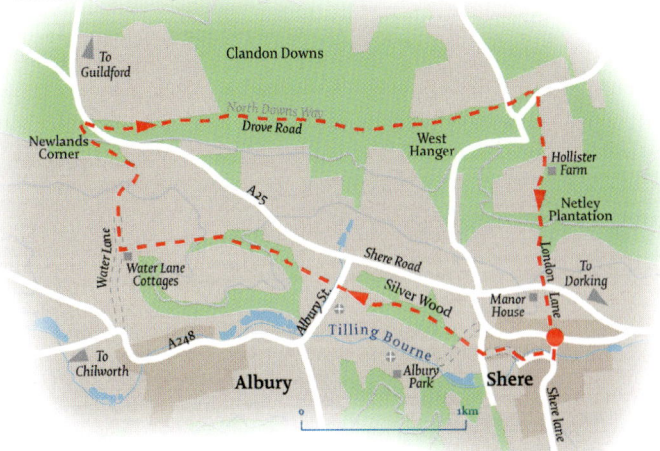

field down past Albury Park's church on the left and across the A248. The footpath continues ahead up the right-hand field edge, over a stile and through woodland, before leading past a timber yard and up to a cottage, Timbercroft, at a bridleway junction. Keep ahead down the bridleway along the edge of woodland and between fields, then down past Water Lane Cottages to the junction with Water Lane.

A right turn up Water Lane, which soon becomes a stony byway, takes you uphill fairly steeply for 1km to the junction with the North Downs Way at Newlands Corner, where there is a car park with a café and toilets, and some long views southwards over the Surrey Hills.

The onward route turns right onto the North Downs Way, crosses the A25, where a little care is needed with the traffic, and continues through woodland with glimpses of views through the trees on a mostly level track. After 1.8km head over a crosspaths and carry on through West Hanger Nature Reserve to reach the car park at Staple Lane. The North Downs Way continues over the lane for 200m before making a short dogleg right, then left along a track for 400m to the bridleway junction by Hollister Farm.

Here, you leave the North Downs Way and keep ahead on the bridleway, the right-hand of two paths, which skirts along the right-hand edge of woodland and then drops down alongside a field and through Netley Plantation to the A25. Join the sunken byway of London Lane on the left (muddy at times) which heads under the road and descends in 400m back into Shere.

Peaslake and Pitch Hill

Distance 6km **Time** 1 hour 45 **Terrain** woodland tracks and paths, with a steady climb up to Pitch Hill **Map** OS Explorer 145 **Access** bus from Guildford and Cranleigh to Peaslake village, 350m from the start

A classic woodland walk is topped off with fine views from Pitch Hill.

The walk starts from Hurtwood car park 2, situated along Walking Bottom, 350m southwest of the village of Peaslake. The Hurtwood is an extensive area of commonland in private ownership. There are 14 free car parks and people are welcome to walk and ride throughout the woodland, according to a 'right of air and exercise' first granted in 1926 by the Bray family of Shere. The area has become very popular with walkers, as well as with mountain-bikers and trailrunners, and can get very busy at peak times. In Peaslake itself you will find the Village Stores and The Hurtwood Inn. The village is also linked with the Long Distance Walkers Association, whose founding members used the village's post office to advertise their early marathon-style walks. This route is somewhat gentler.

Head out of the top of the car park through the gate and take the bridleway along the main track which rises steadily up the wooded valley floor. Ignore paths off left or right and carry on for just under 1.5km to a prominent fork with a public footpath at a marker post. Bear left onto the footpath which takes you more steeply up the left-hand valley. After 500m, as the gradient eases, continue over a crosspaths and in another 200m the footpath joins a bridleway which curves to the right up to the triangulation pillar on Pitch Hill. A topograph, a little down to the left, marks out the views east to Holmbury Hill, south to the South Downs and west to Gibbet Hill and Black Down.

The onward route turns right down the main path and contours a little round the

PEASLAKE AND PITCH HILL

◀ Ewhurst Windmill

hill before descending past a quarry to Hurtwood car park 3. Here, head across the road and take the Greensand Way footpath up past Mill Cottage – ignore the holloway off to the right – over a stile and up steeply through the trees to a track by Ewhurst Windmill, a tower mill built in the middle of the 19th century. It used to have four sails but has now been converted to residential use. The Greensand Way keeps left past the windmill and into the wood beyond, before descending down to the road, with Hurtwood car park 4 across the road on the left.

Cross Winterfold Heath Road and opposite the car park turn right, off the Greensand Way, onto the bridleway which leads downhill through deciduous woodland before passing through a gate into the mixed plantation of Winterfold Wood. After another 300m the bridleway track curves right over first a footpath crosspaths and then a bridleway crosspaths, after which it heads up over a rise through deciduous woodland once more and down to Hound House Road.

Across the road take the bridleway which heads WNW through Bentley Copse, past Bentley Copse Activity Centre, up over a rise and down past Peaslake House to Lawbrook Lane. A short dogleg left along the lane, then right takes you onto a path leading through the trees back down to the car park at the start.

Holmbury Hill

Distance 6km **Time** 1 hour 45
Terrain woodland paths and tracks
Map OS Explorer 146 **Access** bus to
Holmbury St Mary (which is on the route)
from Dorking

A longer approach through delightful woodland brings you to the top of one of the Surrey Hills' best-known high points.

The walk starts from Hurtwood car park 14, Lower Holmbury Hill, opposite the entrance to Holmbury St Mary Youth Hostel, which is situated off the B2126 Horsham Road at the top of the single-track Radnor Lane.

At the top of the car park turn left onto the footpath and follow the yellow waymarks through the trees over the rise, down across a prominent dip and up the far side. The footpath soon curves to the right and just after it starts to descend, at a fork, bear left down through the trees past Felday Chapel to Holmbury St Mary.

Go right and head past The Green and The Royal Oak to take the footpath up the lane past the church to a footpath junction.

The Church of St Mary was designed and paid for by the Victorian architect G E Street. When he visited in the 1870s the village was called Felday. He soon returned to live in the village and its name was changed to Holmbury St Mary. Street designed many churches, often favouring the Gothic style, though he is usually associated with the Law Courts in The Strand. The architectural historian Sir Nikolaus Pevsner was not a fan, calling the church the 'perfect example of form without content'.

In the 1920s another frequent visitor was E M Forster, who used his knowledge of the village for the setting of his fictional 'Summerstreet' in his novel *A Room with a View*, though in the 1986 film the village scenes were filmed elsewhere, in Chiddingstone in Kent.

At the footpath junction, turn sharp left and pass above the church before bending right through woodland and descending to Holmbury Hill Road at the southern end of the village, where a right turn brings you up past the King's Head to the junction with Pitland Street.

Here, the route turns right onto the Greensand Way which leads up steps into woodland. This well-waymarked route takes you over a track and up to join a broader track, which heads up past Holmbury cricket club and on for another 300m to a five-way track junction. Here, the Greensand Way turns left up a broad track for 200m and then forks right onto a narrower path more steeply uphill, before dropping down left and circling to the right. The path now heads round the earthworks of Holmbury hillfort up to the top of the hill, where there are some information panels and a topograph to help interpret the views and the history.

The onward route heads to the left of the triangulation pillar, then keeps left at three forks in the path descending northwestwards to a holloway just below Hurtwood car park 1. Turn right for 50m to the top of the holloway and past the car park to a broad six-way track junction.

Here, take the track which continues northwards downhill along the right-hand side of Hurtwood Millennium Pinetum. This broad track descends gently down the forest valley, after 900m heading over a prominent cross-track and continuing down for another 1km to a bridleway T-junction by a pond. Turn right past the pond, follow the bridleway over the rise and then fork left along the edge of the forestry for 100m to return to the car park at the start.

◀ Near the viewpoint on top of Holmbury Hill

Ewhurst

Distance 4.5km **Time** 1 hour 15
Terrain lanes, fields and woodland
Map OS Explorer 145 **Access** bus to
Ewhurst (Bull's Head stop) from
Cranleigh and Gomshall

Take your time with this shorter walk through a nature reserve and over fields near a former Roman settlement.

The walk starts from the northern end of the village of Ewhurst at the crossroads junction of the B2127 with Shere Road, where there is parking around the small green alongside The Street, opposite the Bull's Head Inn.

From the junction head down Wykehurst Lane. This carries a footpath for 600m past cottages and houses and then alongside fields and through woodland to the footpath off left into Sayers Croft Nature Reserve. Yellow arrow waymarks show the way through the trees, down across a stream and up to a stile into fields. Head up over the rise in the first field where you cross the line of a Roman road, an off-shoot of Stane Street which ran from Noviomagus (Chichester) to Londinium and passes nearby on the eastern side of Leith Hill.

On the far side of the field the footpath continues along a fenced section and over a paddock to the driveway of Penquite Farm. Another section of fenced footpath now takes you down past the buildings of Lemans Farm and over a stile into woodland. Continue through the trees on a path (which can be muddy) down to a crosspaths junction with a bridleway.

The route now turns right and heads northwards up the wooded bridleway with the fairways of Cranleigh Golf Club on the left. After 600m you cross over a stream and then a staggered crosspaths, beyond which the bridleway forks right up a rise to a crosspaths. Here, turn right off the bridleway down to a fenced

◀ Bus-stop shelter in Ewhurst

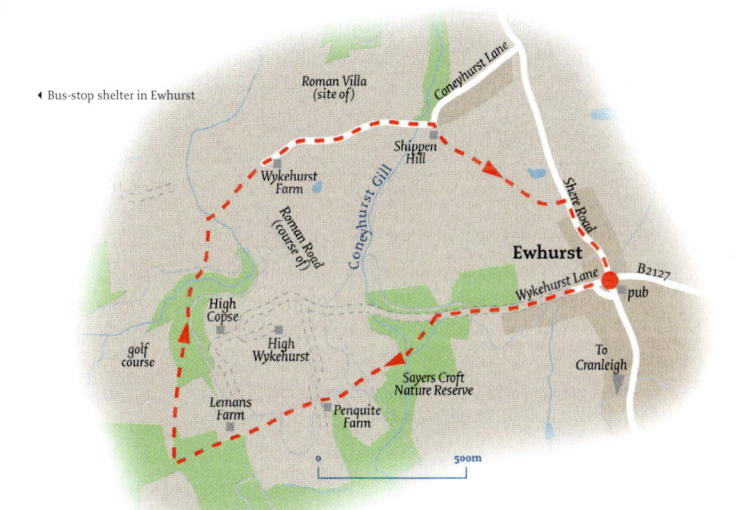

footpath which heads up the left-hand edge of a field, crossing once more over the line of the Roman road, to a gate onto a track.

To the north, at the foot of the slope of Pitch Hill, lies Rapsley Farm where in the 1950s and 1960s a Roman villa dated to the 2nd-4th centuries AD was located and excavated. Archaeologists discovered mosaics and heated rooms in what was possibly an estate of considerable extent. Nearby the remains of what is thought to be a Roman brickworks and tile kiln had already been discovered in the 1930s. Both sites are only a short distance from the Roman road crossed earlier in the walk.

At the track bear right, past farm buildings and then the entrance to Wykehurst Farm, beyond which you continue along the pleasant lane between fields to the houses of Coneyhurst where the lane bends left. Here, take the footpath off right through the gate and past the cottages. In front of Shippen Hill house bear left a short way up a track to a fork in the footpath and branch left through the gate into fields. Head across the top of the first field, aim to the left of the telegraph pole in the second, cross a small third field and then bear to the left in the fourth to reach a stile onto Shere Road on the outskirts of Ewhurst. Here, a right turn along the pavement for 300m takes you back to the start.

Walliswood

Distance 5.5km **Time** 1 hour 30
Terrain lanes, fields and woodland
Map OS Explorer OL34 **Access** bus to
Walliswood from Guildford, Dorking and
Cranleigh (intermittent service)

This little jewel of a country walk makes its way along lanes and byways, through woodland and over fields.

The walk starts from the southern end of the village of Walliswood, at the junction of Horsham Road with Froggetts Lane by The Scarlett Arms pub, where there is a roadside parking area. The sign of the Scarlett Arms prominently displays its motto *suis stat viribus* (one stands by one's own strength), perhaps just as suitable for a walk as for a pub, though this route is short enough to leave plenty of time to visit beforehand or afterwards.

From the junction head up Froggetts Lane for 500m, signed for Ewhurst, which winds its way past Walliswood Farm. Just past Froggetts Farm, take the footpath off right up the driveway to the gates of Northlands, where the footpath forks off left down a field and through woodland to the byway of Lowerhouse Lane. A right turn up this pleasant wooded byway for 800m takes you up over a slight rise and down to Lower Breache Road.

Here, turn right onto the footpath past Lyefield House and up the driveway for 250m, with views northwards towards Pitch Hill and Holmbury Hill, to the gate of Lowerhouse Farm. A footpath heads off left over a stile and up the field ahead and then into a second field alongside a hedge to the driveway to Mayes Court. Bear right with the footpath down the driveway, with a view left to Leith Hill, and carry on,

◀ The front of The Scarlett Arms in Walliswood

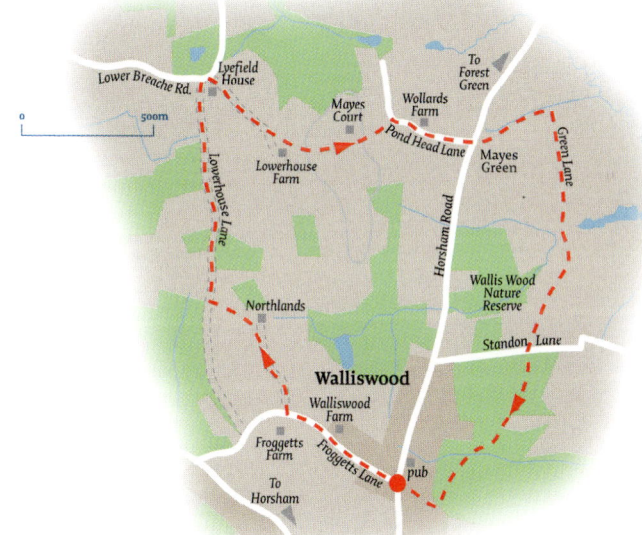

now on a byway, down past Wollards Farm to the road at Mayes Green.

After crossing the road, continue along the byway for 300m, then turn right along the wooded byway of Green Lane. After 400m you cross a small stream and, in another 150m, fork right through a gate onto a footpath. This leads along the edges of two fields to reach a gate onto Standon Lane, with Wallis Wood Nature Reserve away to the right along this section. The woodland reserve is secluded and unfrequented, as there is no car park nearby. A variety of woodland flora can be found, including bluebells, orchids, wood anemone and wild daffodil. In addition it's a good place for spotting woodland butterflies, such as the purple emperor and the white admiral.

Cross the lane and follow the waymarked footpath through the woodland for 400m, passing between houses and over two driveways, to a footbridge over a stream. Continue ahead for another 300m, up steps, along a fenced section and on to a crosspaths on the far side of the wood. A right turn by the edge of the wood takes you along the backs of houses to Horsham Road opposite Froggetts Lane and the start.

Cottage at Pinehurst at the foot of Box Hill ▶

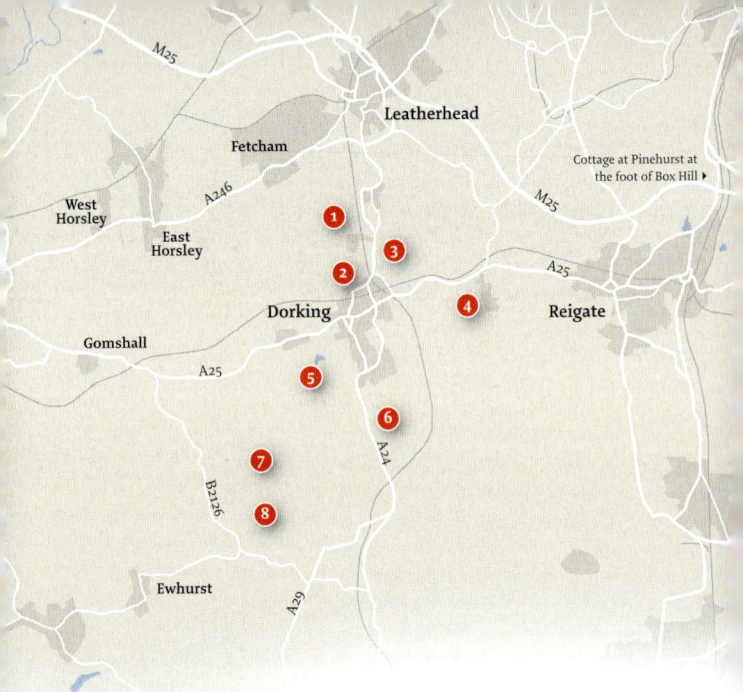

This section contains some of the best known and most frequently visited locations in the Surrey Hills. The old market town of Dorking is situated between Guildford and Reigate on the A25 at the crossroads with the A24 London to Worthing road. Except to its southeast, the town is surrounded by the high ground and steep slopes of the North Downs and the Greensand Ridge. To the northeast lies Box Hill and the chalk downs above Mickleham. Westwards across the Mole Valley rise the slopes and plateau-like woods and fields of Norbury Park and Ranmore Common. Heading southwards over Abinger Common the ground becomes increasingly covered by trees until a final steepening through the woods leads to the high vantage point of Leith Hill.

Some of the most satisfying walking the region has to offer is to be found in this part of the Surrey Hills. The steep slopes and higher ground lend themselves to longer and more strenuous routes, where ascents can be surprisingly sharp and on the higher ground there is a sense of being, if not in hillcountry, then at least removed enough from urban centres to gain a sense of space.

Dorking

1 **Mole Valley and Norbury Park** 64
Meander with the River Mole and enjoy meadows and woodland before returning along a bridleway

2 **Ranmore Common** 66
Follow the North Downs Way to take in some of the best views in the Surrey Hills

3 **Box Hill** 68
Take a longer winding route up the much-loved summit managed by the National Trust

4 **Brockham and Betchworth** 70
Loop around the parkland between two pretty villages either side of the River Mole

5 **Westcott and Squire's Great Wood** 72
Wander along an ancient byway and over heathland on this rural loop

6 **Holmwood Common** 74
Enjoy the easy-to-follow undulating trails in this popular National Trust-owned woodland

7 **Friday Street and Leith Hill** 76
Make the most of the surrounding countryside on this longer hike to the well-known viewpoint

8 **Leith Hill Woodland Trail** 78
Be prepared for a steep but short climb to enjoy the wonderful view from this National Trust property

Mole Valley and Norbury Park

Distance 6km **Time** 1 hour 45
Terrain riverside fields, woodland, with two steep climbs **Map** OS Explorer 146
Access bus to Burford Bridge from Dorking and Leatherhead; train to Box and Westhumble Station from Dorking and Leatherhead

This short walk explores a variety of landscapes – riverside meadows, working woodland and views along the Mole Gap.

The walk starts from Box and Westhumble Station, north of Dorking. Parking at the station is only for railway-users so, if arriving by car, one alternative start point is the small car park near the top of narrow Crabtree Lane, 1km back along the route; the other is near Burford Bridge and the A24, where there is some roadside parking on the B2209 Old London Road and also a larger car park at Ryka's Café (check closing times). From here you can follow the Thames Down Link path for 800m along the pavement to Burford Bridge, under the A24 via the subway and along Westhumble Street to the station.

The first part of the route follows the River Mole as it winds its course northwards towards the North Downs. The river has cut a cleft in these hills that is known as the Mole Gap, beyond which it flows towards Leatherhead and on to join the Thames. For millennia this gap has been a conduit for humans and animals; now the A24 dual carriageway squeezes past Mickleham, while the railway tunnels its way under Norbury Park. Norbury Park House is also clearly visible on top of the downs. The mansion was built in the 18th century and in the middle of the 19th century the owner allowed the railway to be built through the park, so long as it was, as far as possible, hidden from view. In 1930 the estate was sold to Surrey County Council and today it is under the management of Surrey Wildlife Trust.

MOLE VALLEY AND NORBURY PARK

◀ Looking north to Norbury Park

Turn left out of the station over the railway bridge and take the footpath off right alongside the railway into fields, with a view to Norbury Park House up on the ridge ahead. The footpath keeps to the right-hand edge and crosses the River Mole on a footbridge, before forking left across the next field. (These fields can be very muddy when wet). At the far end of the field bear right along a lane to the buildings of Cowslip Farm where the route turns left, signed for Leatherhead, along the farm track and over the River Mole again. You now pass to the left of Lodge Farm and continue up to a small picnic area just before the woodland of Norbury Park.

Go through the gate into the trees and bear right uphill through beech and oak woodland for 600m to a bridleway junction at the top of the rise just out of the trees. A left turn up the bridleway takes you steeply uphill past a communications mast to a path junction at the top of the rise, where a short detour left is possible through Centenary Copse to a viewpoint. Continue ahead down the bridleway alongside the fence past an entrance of Norbury Park, then down across a dip and up to a tarmac driveway. A left turn uphill for 300m brings you to Norbury Park Sawmill where there is a picnic area.

The onward route forks left in front of the picnic area along the track past the sawmill and after 600m passes a path off left to another picnic area, with a viewpoint over the Mole Valley to Box Hill and the Mole Gap. A little further along the track, a bridleway joins from the right and soon starts to descend. Where the track bends left make sure you fork right to stay on the bridleway, which heads up over a rise and down to the small car park by Crabtree Lane. From here turn left down the narrow tree-lined lane for 1km to return to the start.

Ranmore Common

Distance 7.5km **Time** 2 hours 15
Terrain lanes and woodland tracks and paths, with a steady climb up to Ranmore Common **Map** OS Explorer 146
Access bus to Burford Bridge from Dorking and Leatherhead; train to Box Hill and Westhumble Station from Dorking and Leatherhead

The slopes above the Mole Valley have some of the best vantage points you will find in the Surrey Hills.

The walk starts from Box Hill and Westhumble Station, north of Dorking. (For information on nearby parking at Burford Bridge, see the Mole Valley and Norbury Park walk.) Turn left out of the station over the railway bridge and head up Chapel Lane for 200m. At the top of the rise, just beyond Pilgrims Way, a narrow footpath heads off left between houses, down across Adlers Lane and between more houses to a field gate. Cross the narrow field and head into the woodland beyond to a prominent crosspaths, where you can turn right onto the North Downs Way.

The well-waymarked trail heads uphill and then bends left to join a tarmac track over a bridleway junction (where the return route comes in), up through the wood and round a right bend. Here, you come out of the trees and there are great views to Box Hill and, a little further on, over Dorking and round to Leith Hill, where its tower is visible on the skyline in a gap in the trees, with Denbies' vineyards spread over the slopes below. The North Downs Way keeps up the tarmac track for another 800m, passing through two road gates to a bridleway junction in front of Denbies house. The name Denby originates from an old farmer, but the mansion was built in the middle of the 19th century by Thomas Cubitt. He was also responsible for commissioning Sir Gilbert Scott to design Ranmore Church. Its spire is a landmark which can be seen for miles around and neighbours at the time referred to it as 'Cubitt's Finger'.

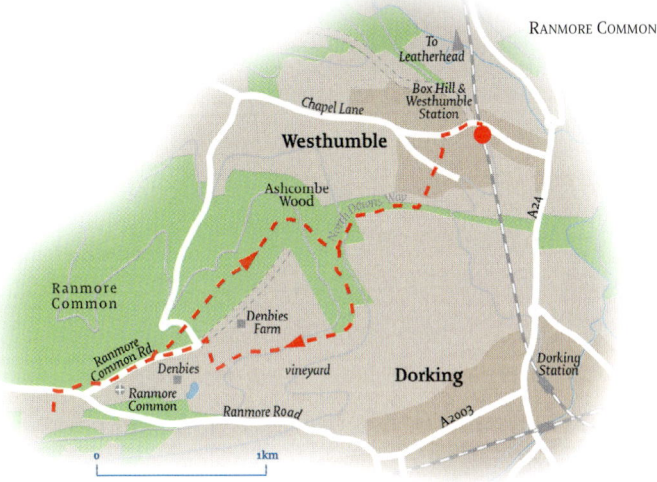

Turn right up to a track junction and then left up to Ranmore Common Road by North Lodge. Here the North Downs Way keeps ahead along a grassy track on the right of the road, after 300m passing the first of two bridleways off right, which marks the return route. However, it is well worth continuing for another 600m, past Ranmore Church, up the track through the trees and on to Denbies car park across the road beside Ranmore Common, where you can take in an even wider view from Steers Field beyond. There are also some picnic benches here.

Retrace steps past the church and take the second bridleway off left into the trees. The narrow winding bridleway can be muddy at times as it heads down over Ranmore Common Road and then gradually descends for 750m through the woods and across two shallow dips to a junction where a path comes in from the right. Continue along the bridleway and make sure you keep right at two forks in the path in quick succession. The bridleway now bends to the right and descends more steeply down over a path and track junction, before heading steeply down a stonier track for 200m to bring you out onto the North Downs Way.

From here, turn left and retrace the waymarks of the outward route down the tarmac track, round the right bend and on for 400m to the prominent crosspaths. A marker post for Westhumble points you left off the North Downs Way over the narrow field, between houses to Chapel Lane and back down to the start.

◀ Looking south over Denbies Vineyard towards Dorking

Box Hill

Distance 5.75km **Time** 1 hour 45
Terrain woodland and valley paths, open downland; cumulative ascent 225m
Map OS Explorer 146 **Access** bus to Burford Bridge from Dorking and Leatherhead; train to Box Hill and Westhumble Station, 800m from the start

A longer approach via Juniper Bottom brings you to the most popular high point in the Surrey Hills.

The walk starts from Burford Bridge north of Dorking by the A24, where there is some roadside parking on the B2209 Old London Road and also a popular car park and picnic site at Ryka's Café (check gate closing times). If arriving by train you can follow the Thames Down Link path for 800m from Box Hill and Westhumble Station along Westhumble Street, under the A24 via the subway and along the pavement to Burford Bridge.

Many visitors to Box Hill wonder about the origin of its name and are not surprised to learn that it comes from the box trees that used to grow abundantly on its slopes and supplied the needs of 18th-century wood-engravers in London. However, names change and when the antiquarian and historian William Camden was researching *Britannia*, his 16th-century topographical survey of Great Britain and Ireland, the chalk hill was known simply as White Hill. This name still survives for the hill immediately to the north above Mickleham.

From the entrance to the car park at Ryka's Café, cross the B2209 and turn left onto the Thames Down Link path which heads uphill through a gate and then keeps left at a fork to continue parallel to the B2209 up to the junction with Zig Zag Road. Continue up the pavement of the B2209 for 250m to the top of the rise, where a footpath heads steeply off to the right up the wooded driveway past Pinehurst Lodge. Keep on up the driveway past Little Pinehurst and bear left onto a level path through two gates into National Trust woodland. The footpath contours through the trees for 200m before dropping fairly steeply to the left,

◀ Looking up the
Burford Spur of
Box Hill

down to the bridleway in Juniper Bottom.

The route now turns right onto the bridleway track which winds its way steadily up the valley past many a juniper tree and amongst other species, including beech, hazel, ash, silver birch, larch, chestnut, hawthorn, cherry and, of course, box. You pass through a gate and then a clearing on the left, beyond which the path gradually steepens to reach a track junction. Head over the junction and continue along the now level bridleway through woodland dominated by yew for 500m to reach the edge of Box Hill village. Cross the road and turn right onto the roadside path for 150m, after which you can dogleg left, then right to join the North Downs Way for 500m to reach the triangulation pillar and topograph at the summit. This is a memorial to Leopold Salomons of Norbury Park who donated the land to the National Trust in 1914.

Once you have taken in the view to Leith Hill and beyond, bear right up past the car park to Box Hill Café and toilets, where a large fingerpost points the way to Box Hill Fort, situated to the rear of the café. The fort was one of a chain built in the 19th century along the North Downs and there is a helpful information panel to explain the history.

Continue past the fort down the flinty bridleway and in 100m fork left onto the Walkers' Path along Burford Spur, which descends initially on a chalky path and then down a broad grass slope, with views left to Ranmore Common and ahead through the Mole Gap towards London. At the bottom of the spur by Zig Zag Road, turn left and retrace your steps back down the Thames Down Link path to Burford Bridge.

Brockham and Betchworth

Distance 4km **Time** 1 hour
Terrain fields and woods; muddy sections in wet conditions **Map** OS Explorer 146
Access bus to Brockham from Guildford, Dorking, Redhill and Horsham

Take a little stroll between two pretty Surrey villages, with a choice of pubs and a café for refreshment.

The walk starts from the village of Brockham, where there is parking around The Green. The village has two pubs, The Royal Oak and The Inn on The Green, as well as The Reading Room Café located at the village hall.

From The Green walk along Middle Street past the church and turn left along Wheelers Lane for just under 400m past houses to Dodds Park. Here, look out for the footpath off left along a track past allotments to a field gate. Head along the laid path beside the first field to a gate into a second field, where the path divides. Take the left fork and keep ahead up across the field towards Oldpark Wood, with views right to Leith Hill and back towards Box Hill.

Follow the field path along the edge of the wood and turn left with it to a gate into parkland. Head across the parkland beyond, passing Betchworth Diamond Jubilee Beacon off on the right, and bear a little left down past a dozen large oak trees and over a path junction to the southern corner of Dendy's Wood. The path bends left here down along the edge of the wood to a gate into the trees and then brings you down to a footbridge across a small stream, with the River Mole away to the left. Head up the far side (muddy at times) out of the wood and across a field to Snowerhill Road. A left turn over the narrow bridge and the River Mole takes you along a footway around the bend and beside the wall of Betchworth House into Betchworth.

In the middle of the village, opposite the junction of Wonham Lane and The Dolphin Inn, the onward route turns left onto the Greensand Way, which is followed for the rest of the walk. Head through the gated archway into the churchyard and past St Michael's Church, inside which are some panels outlining its history and plenty of interesting memorials. Fans of the 1994 romantic comedy *Four Weddings and a Funeral* will be delighted to know the church featured in the film; Angus and Laura tied the knot here in the first scene. At the far end of the churchyard, the Greensand Way continues for the next 1km along a track beside woodland and then between fields, with a view right to Box Hill, before passing gardens above the River Mole and heading up to a bridleway junction.

A left turn with the Greensand Way down the bridleway track alongside Poland Woods takes you past a pillbox on the left and over the River Mole again. Follow the tarmac walkway back up to the houses of Brockham and bear right to return to The Green.

◀ Houses around The Green in the village of Brockham

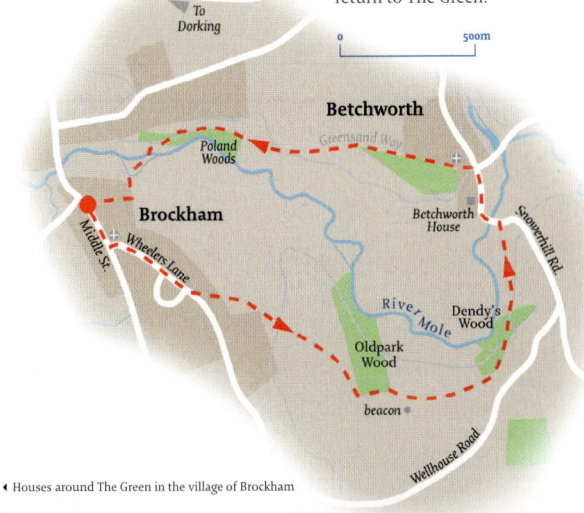

Westcott and Squire's Great Wood

Distance 8km **Time** 2 hours 15
Terrain lanes, fields and woods
Map OS Explorer 146 **Access** bus from Dorking and Guildford

Stride out over fields, heathland and along an ancient byway from a village with a vibrant history.

The walk starts from the western end of the village of Westcott, below the church at the junction of the A25 Guildford Road with Heath Rise and Westcott Heath. Parking is available alongside the A25 through the village and up Westcott Heath by Holy Trinity Church (except Sunday mornings during church services when traffic cones are put out).

Head up Heath Rise and at the top turn left onto a footpath and the route of the Greensand Way, which heads up behind houses and joins a fenced path that makes its way up over a rise and down to cottages on Milton Street at the eastern edge of the village.

Here, a right turn off the Greensand Way takes you along Milton Street, which carries a bridleway, beside Milton Brook past houses and along a woodland track, leading you between partially hidden fishing lakes to a field gate. The bridleway continues along the right-hand field edge for 150m, where it forks off left over the middle of the field. Leave the bridleway at this point and continue ahead along the field edge on a footpath which then heads up through a copse of woodland, across a small stream and up one more field to meet Logmore Lane.

WESTCOTT AND SQUIRE'S GREAT WOOD

Across the lane, follow the bridleway along the winding driveway for 600m up to Squire's Farm, where the bridleway circles to the left around the buildings to a bridleway junction in Squire's Great Wood. Here, dogleg left for 200m to a fork and then right to ascend more steeply up through the plantation, across a track and up to the byway of Wolvens Lane at the top.

The route now turns right along the pleasant byway for just under 2km, rising gently up through the woodland plantations, past a triangulation pillar and then downhill with intermittent views through the trees. At a sharp left bend, turn right onto a footpath which carries the Greensand Way fairly steeply down through Rookery Wood for 250m to a stile onto a bridleway leading down to houses on Rookery Drive. Until it was demolished in 1968, a large country house, The Rookery, stood near here. Its most famous inhabitant was the radical thinker Thomas Malthus, best known for his 1798 *Essay on the Principle of Population*, who was born and educated at home here.

◀ On Rookery Drive near the end of the route

A right turn now takes you past some pretty cottages by the Pipp Brook and down to the junction with the A25. Turn right onto a footpath which climbs up through Westcott Heath woods, over a lane and along a grassy clearing, with houses on the right, to Westcott Heath Lane just above the church. From here, a left turn onto the path on the right-hand side of the sunken lane will take you back down past the church to the start.

Holmwood Common

Distance 5km **Time** 1 hour 15
Terrain woodland paths and tracks
Map OS Explorer 146 **Access** no public transport to the start

This relaxing short walk is particularly splendid when the trees are cloaked in spring or autumn leaves.

Holmwood Common is situated to the south of Dorking and comprises 650 acres of woodland. This route follows the National Trust's waymarked circular trail around the wooded common on undulating laid paths and tracks. There are five car parks located around the edge of the common and this walk starts from the southeastern corner of the common at Fourwents Blackbrook car park, off Blackbrook Road near the junction with Mill Road.

The four other car parks are Fourwents Mill Road car park on the southern side of Fourwents Pond at the eastern end of Mill Road, Mill Road car park at the southwestern corner of the common by the A24, Inholms car park to the north at the end of Inholms Lane, and Scamells car park off Blackbrook Road to the east. All have a path linking to the circular trail.

Walk out of the back of Fourwents Blackbrook car park, signed to the Circular Trail, past Fourwents Pond and over a footbridge before turning right into woodland, forking right after 150m to reach the circular trail, marked by discs with an orange arrow.

A left turn takes you onto a gravel track leading gently up out of the woodland past Eutrie House, beyond which the trail dives back into woodland to a track junction and turns right over a rise and down past the entrances to Holly House and Braeside. A little further on, fork left past cottages in a clearing to Mill Bottom, where the path from Mill Road car park comes in. Keep ahead past The Mill

HOLMWOOD COMMON

◀ Fourwents Pond

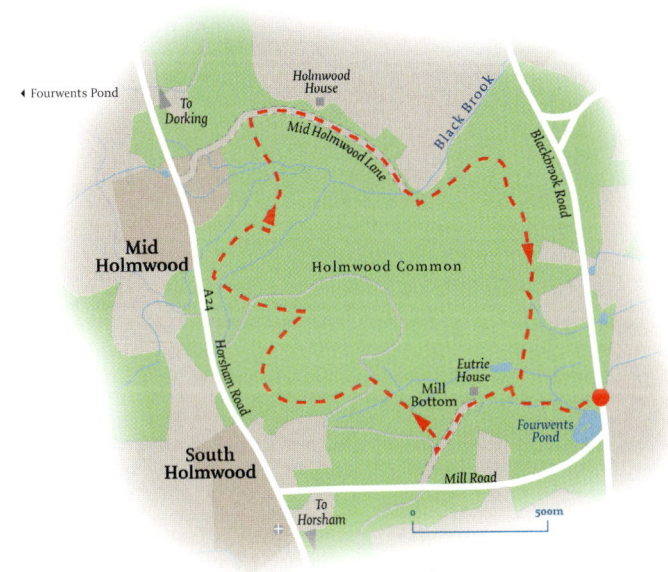

Cottage where the track rises and bends left out of the trees and up round to the right, over a bridleway and past the Old Football Pitch, to reach a viewpoint to Ranmore Common, visible on the skyline ridge over the trees.

From here, the trail bends left and descends towards the A24 before turning right and continuing downhill. The trail bends to the right, turns sharp left and descends to cross a stream before heading gently up on a meandering path to a track junction with a path to Inholms car park and North Holmwood.

The circular trail turns right and takes you along the track of Mid Holmwood Lane past houses and then the red-brick Holmwood House, beyond which you continue down the track for 400m to cottages and a footbridge by the ford over Black Brook. Head over the footbridge and up into the woodland a little where a marker post shows the way along the second path on the left.

The trail now heads uphill, curves to the right and crosses a bridleway at the high point, with Scamells car park off to the left. From here the trail meanders its way downhill over a staggered crosspaths before rising briefly again past two small pools. In another 100m, at the right-hand bend, look out for the marker post for the path back to Fourwents Blackbrook car park and the start.

Friday Street and Leith Hill

Distance 8km **Time** 2 hours 15
Terrain woodland paths and tracks, with a steady ascent of 200m up Leith Hill
Map OS Explorer 146 **Access** no public transport to the start

Begin from the secluded hamlet of Friday Street for a longer approach through woodland to Leith Hill.

The walk starts from the hamlet of Friday Street located 2km south of the A25 Guildford Road at Friday Street car park a little above the hamlet. The hamlet's name is thought to originate from a combined association with the Norse goddess Freya and the proximity of Stane Street, the Roman road from Noviomagus (Chichester) to London.

Another local religious association is with Stephen Langton, commemorated in the name of the hamlet's former pub. Langton was born here in the 12th century and became Archbishop of Canterbury. The Victorian novelist Martin Tupper wrote a romanticised account of how the young Langton and his cousin Alice, his boyhood love, were attacked by bad Prince John, who afterwards became bad King John. Many years later, after Alice has become a nun and he has become archbishop in exile, Langton has his revenge against King John, by being first witness to the signing of Magna Carta, and is reunited with Alice while celebrating mass at nearby St Martha's.

From the car park take the path to the left out of the rear of the car park parallel with the road and head down to the Mill Pond in Friday Street. Continue past the head of the pond and on the far side, take the footpath off right which heads up through the woodland of Severells Copse, over the rise and across two lanes. The footpath now starts to descend and, in 100m, forks right down a sunken path into the hamlet of Broadmoor, where you

◀ On the final approach to the top of Leith Hill

turn left down to the lane.

A left turn down the lane takes you to a track junction after 100m where the Greensand Way heads off right, signed for Warren Farm. This waymarked route takes you up the wooded track past Henman Bunkhouse and, 300m beyond, forks right through woodland to Warren Farm. Here, the path narrows and continues gently uphill for just over 1.5km, steepening as it approaches a prominent track junction. Turn right up the steep final slope to the top of Leith Hill with its tower, kiosk café and views. (To visit the top of the tower check seasonal opening times on the National Trust's website.)

Continuing, the Greensand Way drops down towards Starveall Corner car park on a broad path through the woods. After just over 400m, pass a path off left (for the circular Woodland Trail) and a short way on ignore the path off right (for the car park) and continue down to Leith Hill Road. The Greensand Way now crosses the road, drops downhill past a small parking area and forks right along a track after 200m. Near the top of the second small rise, where the Greensand Way turns off left to High Ashes Farm, carry on ahead to emerge on Leith Hill Road.

Here, turn left to follow the road for 300m past the lane leading to Broadmoor. Round the left bend, take the bridleway branching off right down through the beechwoods of Abinger Bottom to houses by Abinger Common Road. Dogleg left down the road for 100m, then right to carry on along the bridleway for 600m down to Friday Street. Follow the lane through the hamlet and past the former Stephen Langton Inn to the Mill Pond below the car park.

Leith Hill Woodland Trail

Distance 4km **Time** 1 hour 15
Terrain woodland paths and tracks
Map OS Explorer 146 **Access** no public transport to the start

This short but tough little route involves a bracing ascent of nearly 200m to gain the top of Leith Hill.

The walk starts from the National Trust Rhododendron Wood car park off Tanhurst Lane located to the north of Leith Hill Place. This is a shorter route to the top of Leith Hill than the walk from Friday Street but it still includes a steep ascent. An alternative start is from the smaller Windy Gap car park, along the route on Abinger Road. This walk follows the National Trust's waymarked Woodland Trail and passes near to the entrance to Leith Hill Place on its way to the top of Leith Hill.

Leith Hill Place and Leith Hill Tower are both now owned and managed by the National Trust. The house is the former home of the Wedgwood family and the Vaughan Williams family. It was the composer Ralph Vaughan Williams who gave the house to the National Trust in 1944. The tower is open to the public (check seasonal opening times on the National Trust's website) and was built in 1765 by Richard Hull, a former resident of Leith Hill Place. He wanted to build a prospect house from which people could enjoy the 'glory of the English countryside'. When he died in 1772 his request to be buried underneath it was granted. Despite being extended 100 years later, the tower gradually fell into disrepair and Richard Hull was largely forgotten until, in the 1980s, his remains were discovered during excavations of the foundations.

The Woodland Trail heads out of the

LEITH HILL WOODLAND TRAIL

◀ Leith Hill Tower

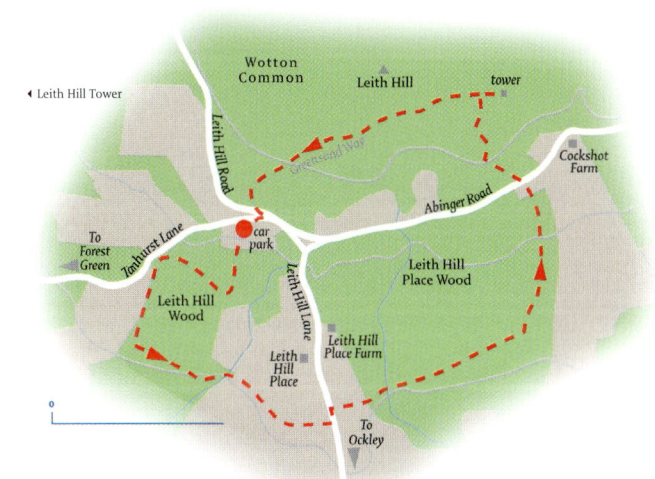

bottom right of the car park downhill over a bridleway, then bends round to the right and climbs gently to a track junction. Turn left twice in quick succession and descend through the woods for 200m, where the trail turns left in front of a wooden barrier and heads gently down to a fork with the Etherley Farm Loop. The Woodland Trail keeps left up through the trees before bending right and crossing the parkland below Leith Hill Place where there are extensive views southwards all the way to the South Downs and south-westwards to Black Heath and Gibbet Hill.

At Abinger Road you make a short dogleg left uphill (the entrance to Leith Hill Place itself is further up the road), then right to continue on a narrower path down along the walled gardens of Leith Hill Place and uphill to the left along an avenue of lime trees. The trail now heads over a track junction and up a straighter track before bending left and rising more steeply up into the trees to Abinger Road, where a short dogleg left, then right takes you through Windy Gap car park. You now face two sets of steep steps for the final climb up through woodland, at the top of which the trail bears right up to the tower at the top of Leith Hill.

From the tower, the Woodland Trail heads gently down the western slope of the hill on a broad path to reach a marker post after just over 400m. Here, the trail turns left onto a narrower path more steeply down through denser woodland to a sharp left turn above a deep holloway and down to Leith Hill Road. Cross the road and turn right along Tanhurst Lane for 100m to return to Rhododendron Wood car park.

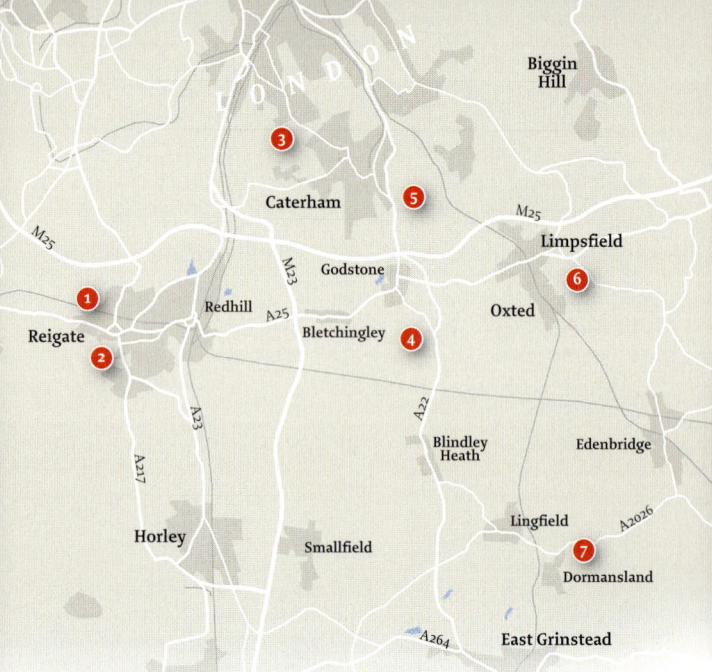

The easternmost section of the Surrey Hills stretches in a narrow meandering strip either side of the M25 motorway from just west of Reigate to the county border with Kent beyond Oxted. Cutting this area in two are the A23 and the M23, the main routes heading south past Redhill towards the coast at Brighton. The current boundary review of the AONB proposes to widen this corridor to include a larger area on the London side of the North Downs and the countryside to the south of the A25.

The walks in this section are spread throughout this anticipated extended area, and also included is the outlying pocket of the AONB in the southeast corner of the county near Lingfield. What this eastern part lacks in geographical spread, it in part makes up for in hidden delights found close to towns and major routes. Paths over tucked-away folds in the downs, unexpected expanses of commons and still picturesque village centres gathered around still open village greens are all readily found by those venturing away from the more popular central and western parts of the Surrey Hills.

Summer fields below Hopgarden Wood south of Godstone ▶

Reigate and the east

1 Colley Hill — 82
Ignore the motorway hum and revel instead in the views from this high point on the edge of Reigate

2 Skimmington and Reigate Park — 84
Enjoy an easy loop around the parkland and wooded heath on the edge of town

3 Farthing Downs and Happy Valley — 86
Take in a down-top view of distant London's skyscrapers before exploring a delightful grassland valley

4 Godstone and Tilburstow Hill — 88
Follow in the footprints of Surrey's original rambler on this easy-going rural circuit

5 Woldingham and Marden Park — 90
Buckle up for a rollercoaster circuit with city views in the folds of the North Downs

6 Limpsfield and The Chart — 92
Starting from a village packed with notable buildings, take a rolling hike through woods and over heathland

7 Dormansland and Dry Hill — 94
Explore the southeastern corner of Surrey where the county meets Kent and East Sussex

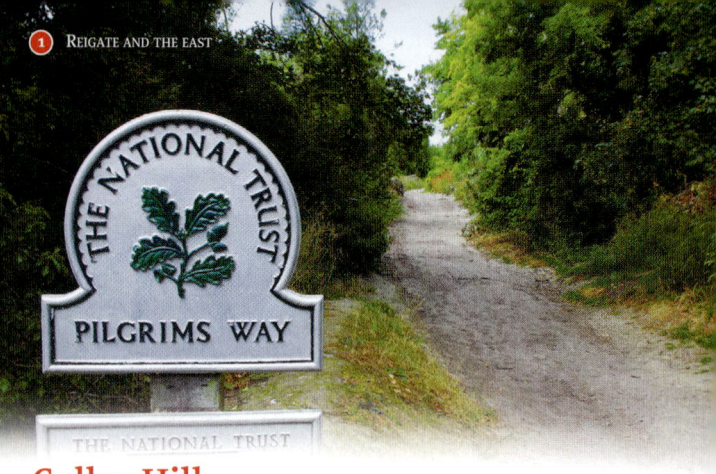

Colley Hill

Distance 7km **Time** 2 hours
Terrain footpaths, lanes, woods and open hillside, with an ascent of 180m up Colley Hill **Map** OS Explorer 146 **Access** no public transport to the start

From Reigate Heath, head for the well-known memorial on top of Colley Hill with sweeping views southwards.

The walk starts from Reigate Heath car park, situated to the west of Reigate, 500m off the A25 down Flanchford Road towards the village of Skimmington.

Walk back up the side of Reigate Heath alongside Flanchford Road to the A25 and turn right along the pavement for just over 200m. At the end of the row of bungalows set back from the road, cross over the road and take the footpath to the left of Alexandra Gate. The fenced footpath rises up between houses and gardens and continues into Coppice Lane byway and over the railway. Carry on along the byway lane over the rise and down to where the lane bends to the left. Leave the lane here and keep ahead uphill with the byway, which forks left after 100m by a private drive and narrows as it rises up past a house to a path T-junction. You now turn right onto the Pilgrims Way for 300m along the bottom of the wooded slope to a lane and some houses.

Here, a left turn takes you up steps into woodland, where you'll need to brace yourself for a stiff climb up through the trees on a chalky tree-rooted path. After exiting the woodland, join a bridleway coming up from the right by a bench just below a memorial stone, with fine views back over Reigate and south over the Weald. The route continues up less steeply through the trees and beside railings to a gate, where the bridleway bends left up to the track along the top of

COLLEY HILL

◀ Looking back along the route to the south of Colley Hill

Colley Hill – you can detour right to see the Inglis Memorial, a neoclassical octagonal rotunda, which commemorates Sir Robert Inglis' gift of the land of Colley Hill to the Borough of Reigate in 1909.

At the top, bear left along the broad track which carries the North Downs Way up past a brick watertower and round to the left over the very top of the hill. The M25 is away on the right through the trees but the sound of traffic is compensated for by the extensive views. The onward route keeps on along the North Downs Way down to a gate and along a wooded track for 250m to a driveway. Here, the North Downs Way turns left to briefly follow the driveway past a house and then left again in front of house-gates to drop steeply downhill through woodland before bending back right down to a crosspaths. Leave the North Downs Way as it turns right here, and keep ahead down the bridleway dropping gently for 750m between fields to join Clifford's Lane, a tarmac byway.

Continue ahead down under the railway and past The Old Manor, beyond which Clifton's Lane leads up past gardens and houses over the rise and down to the A25. A quick dogleg left, then right takes you over the A25 and onto a path over Reigate Heath. Cross the heath and bear a little left down to and through a stand of Scots pine to Flanchford Road and the car park.

Skimmington and Reigate Park

Distance 5.5km **Time** 1 hour 30
Terrain woods, fields and parkland
Map OS Explorer 146 **Access** train from
Guildford, Dorking and Redhill to Reigate
Station, 1km off the route

A contrasting walk leads over wooded heathland to the elegant parkland that lies at the heart of Reigate.

The walk starts from Reigate Heath car park, situated to the west of Reigate, 500m off the A25 down Flanchford Road towards the village of Skimmington. It would also be possible to start halfway along the route in Reigate at Priory Park, which is located in the southern part of the town off Bell Street, where there is also a car park.

From Reigate Heath car park on the south side of Flanchford Road, look for the bridleway which runs along the rear of the car park and turn right onto it to drop gently down through woodland for 300m and past a green of Reigate Heath Golf Club to the junction at the edge of the village of Skimmington. The bridleway heads across the lane and a little way up the track towards Skimmington Castle pub before forking left past the pub and its car park, over the rise and down to a track junction. Bear left along Littleton Lane byway to houses and farm buildings, where the return path comes in on the left, and continue up to Park Lane.

Here, cross the road and take the footpath up steps into woodland and then keep on up over the crosspaths up the steep tree-rooted path ahead. The gradient soon eases and you join the main path leading over the wooded crest of Park Hill, past a viewpoint to Colley Hill on the left through the trees and a detour off right for a view southwards. Once you reach the triangulation pillar by

◀ The façade of The Priory in Priory Park, Reigate

a memorial seat, the route forks right with the main path down through trees to the southeastern corner of the park.

You now turn left and then, ignoring the path descending sharp left, follow the tarmac path along the edge of the park, up over a rise and down towards Bell Street. Head to the left here and walk down the open grass slope into Priory Park towards the large house, now a school but formerly an Augustinian priory founded in the 13th century. Following the Dissolution of the Monasteries it became a private mansion and in the middle of the 20th century the land was bought by Reigate Council and is now a park open to all, with a children's playground, picnic area, café and a lake, which was originally a series of fishponds serving the priory.

At the house, follow the Broadwalk off left past the café and play area and along the tree-lined avenue to the lake. Pass to the right of the lake and follow the path around to the far end, where you take the path off right to Park Lane. Cross the road onto the footpath opposite, which leads past allotments beside a stream before bending left between fields to reach the byway of Littleton Lane. Here, a right turn onto the outward route leads you back down Littleton Lane byway and up through Skimmington to the start.

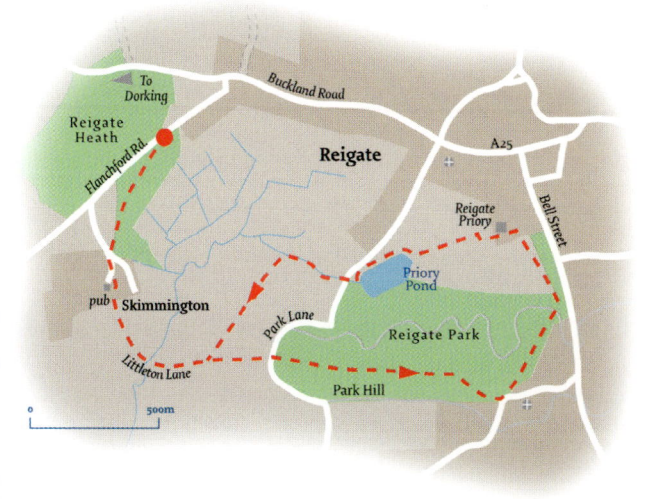

Farthing Downs and Happy Valley

Distance 5km **Time** 1 hour 15
Terrain downland, fields and woods
Map OS Explorer 146 **Access** train from London and Redhill to Coulsdon South, 2km from the start on the London Loop

Views from the top of the downs, a grassland valley and an old church with medieval wall-paintings make this a delight of a walk.

The walk starts from Farthing Downs and New Hill car park. Farthing Downs is owned and managed by the City of London Corporation, which acquired commonland around Coulsdon in the 1880s for the 'recreation and enjoyment of the public'. Today, access to the former commons is still protected, a precious open space within view of the skyscrapers of central London.

Take the path opposite the car park entrance down past Farthing Downs Cottages and bear right onto the bridleway which passes behind the cottages and descends gently down through Devilsden Wood for just over 500m. At the far edge of the woodland, continue ahead into the field and down to the path that runs along the bottom of Happy Valley, whose chalk grassland is home to wild plants and animals, including almost half of all species of butterfly found in Britain.

Bear right here and follow the path gently up the valley bottom through chalk grassland over three fields to reach a crosspaths. A right turn, signed for Leazes Avenue, takes you onto a bridleway up through woodland and alongside a post and rail fence. After 400m, the bridleway continues along a track past houses to a path junction just before Leazes Avenue housing estate. Turn right onto the footpath signed for Chaldon Church,

◀ Looking southeastwards along Happy Valley

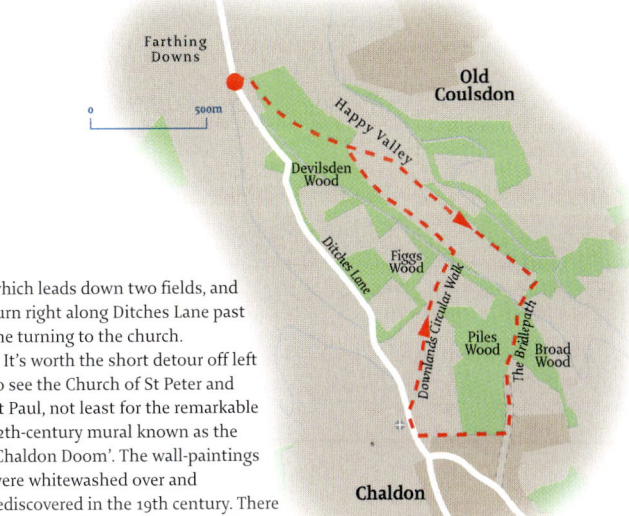

which leads down two fields, and turn right along Ditches Lane past the turning to the church.

It's worth the short detour off left to see the Church of St Peter and St Paul, not least for the remarkable 12th-century mural known as the 'Chaldon Doom'. The wall-paintings were whitewashed over and rediscovered in the 19th century. There are scenes of punishment from the Last Judgement, of which the most graphic is perhaps the two demons holding up a bridge of spikes, with figures representing the sins of avarice, envy, lust, anger, gluttony and sloth. The devil is also seen dragging down souls by a rope to hell, while St Michael guides the righteous to heaven, and more besides.

The onward route back towards Happy Valley heads along Ditches Lane a little further past the church and then takes the footpath off right into fields. The footpath heads up the middle of a field and over the rise, down the far side and through a strip of woodland back into the fields of Happy Valley. Here, turn left and follow the path along the top edge of two fields above the bottom of the valley to reach Devilsden Wood again. Bear left back up the path through the trees to return to the car park on Farthing Downs.

Godstone and Tilburstow Hill

Distance 6.5km **Time** 1 hour 45
Terrain lanes, fields and woodland
Map OS Explorer 146 **Access** bus to
Godstone from Redhill and Oxted

Take the scenic route from one of Surrey's best-known large villages, home of the 'Father of Surrey rambling'.

The walk starts from the centre of Godstone on the High Street by The Green, where there is a public car park (parking limited to three hours). Roadside parking is also available. Godstone is a pretty village built around a large green and was the home of Walker Miles, the 'Father of Surrey rambling'. Born in 1853, his actual name was Edmund Seyfang Taylor. Having inherited the family publishing firm, he used it to publish more than 30 volumes of *Field-Path Rambles* and also founded a number of rambling clubs. This was instrumental in establishing rights of way in a time before definitive maps. He is buried at Church Town, near the end of this route, where his grave is marked by a sarsen stone erected by the Federation of Rambling Clubs.

Walk past the Godstone Pond and along the southern side of The Green to Ivy Mill Lane. Turn left down the lane for 200m and round the right bend. After another 150m take the footpath off left up the driveway of Garston Park. Bear right in front of the house to the top of the driveway. Continue ahead between fields and alongside a wood down to a stile. Climb the right side of the steep field to a stile at the top by a house and keep on through the wood to Rabies Heath Road.

Cross over and head down the lane leading to South Park for just over 100m. Turn left onto the Greensand Way bridleway along the bottom of the woodland on Tilburstow Hill to Tilburstow Road, with intermittent views through the trees to Leith Hill and Black Heath above Haslemere. Continue across

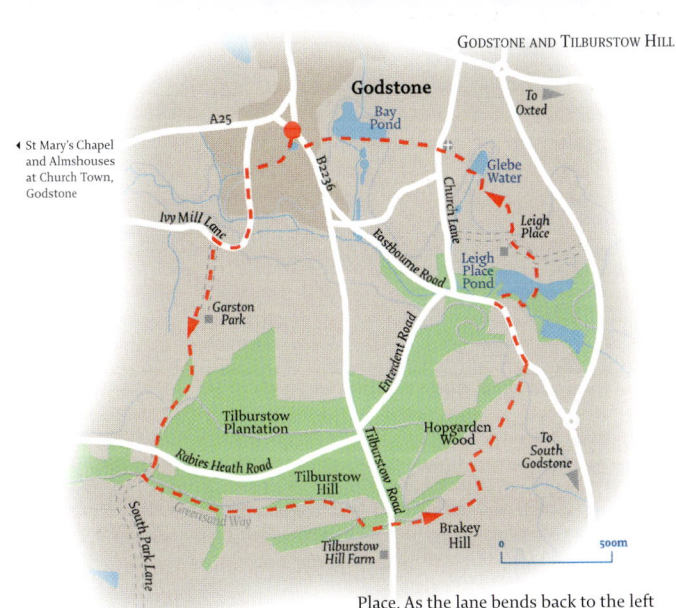

GODSTONE AND TILBURSTOW HILL

◀ St Mary's Chapel and Almshouses at Church Town, Godstone

the road along the bridleway around the east side of Brakey Hill. The bridleway narrows as it leads northwards for 200m. Just before a gate into Hopgarden Wood turn right with the Greensand Way onto a footpath down across fields to the B2236 Eastbourne Road. Turn left along the pavement for 300m to the bend and take the footpath to Tandridge off right down a driveway, which bends to the right and passes over a stream.

Just before the drive bends back to the left make sure you fork left off the Greensand Way onto a fenced path past Leigh Place Pond and up to a bridleway junction on Leigh Place Lane. Turn left and follow the bridleway along the lane and round the right-hand bend past Leigh Place. As the lane bends back to the left keep ahead onto a footpath up the edge of a field for 100m before forking left and then heading downhill. The footpath heads past Glebe Water in a zigzag and up to Church Lane through the cemetery of St Nicholas' Church, where you can find the grave of Walker Miles just down from the east end of the church. This is part of Godstone and is known as Church Town. A little down Church Lane to the left are St Mary's Chapel and Almshouses.

Cross Church Lane and take the footpath by Church House. This heads past Bay Pond, a former hammer pond used in gunpowder manufacture and now managed by the Surrey Wildlife Trust, back to the High Street in Godstone by The Green.

REIGATE AND THE EAST

Woldingham and Marden Park

Distance 9km **Time** 2 hours 30
Terrain parkland, woods and fields
Map OS Explorer 146 **Access** bus to
Woldingham Station from Caterham;
train from London Victoria and
East Grinstead

Enjoy a glorious undulating walk in the folds of the downs just a hop and a skip from London.

The walk starts from Woldingham Railway Station, where there is a car park and roadside parking along Church Road. Woldingham lies in a fold of the North Downs and has long been threatened, but not overwhelmed, by urban expansion. There was a long-running struggle in the 19th century to ensure the railway line was taken under the downs in a tunnel. The 20th century saw the construction nearby of Woldingham Garden Village and then the M25, just over the downs to the south, and there were even provisional plans to build a terminus in Marden Park for a rail link to the Channel Tunnel.

From the station head along Church Road for 500m to Church Road Farm and turn right with the Woldingham Countryside Walk, which is followed for the first part of the route, onto the bridleway over the railway and left along the driveway to the buildings and houses at Marden Park Farm. The bridleway now continues ahead uphill as a track through trees with intermittent views to the left over Woldingham and to the right over Marden Park. After 1km, at a track junction above the buildings of Woldingham School, keep ahead with the Countryside Walk, which circles down round the school before turning left through gates. Continue past the car park and up the chestnut tree-lined driveway to the top at South Lodge.

WOLDINGHAM AND MARDEN PARK

Here, the route forks right, off the Countryside Walk, onto the North Downs Way for the next 600m and descends gently around Winders Hill into Quarry Road. Just past some houses and before the works depot, turn right off the North Downs Way onto Woldingham Parish boundary path. This path heads steeply uphill into woodland up steps, beyond which the gradient eases. At the far edge of the wood cross the top corner of the field beyond and head a little way into the next patch of woodland to a marker post. Fork left with the boundary path up to a stile at the top of the wood.

Bear half-right up the field beyond and then follow the line of a hawthorn hedge over the rise and down to a stile by Paddock Barn depot. The footpath continues for 150m along a fenced section, turns left along a wider path for 250m and then bears right down the long straight track to former Tillingdown Farm, with views ahead to central London. After just over 1km the track bends left around the new houses and then circles back to the right into Tillingdown Lane. Head along the lane for 100m through the housing estate to the bend. Here, leave the lane and keep ahead to a footpath junction behind the houses.

The onward route forks left and leads downhill along a track into woodland and across a grassy valley before a steep climb takes you up the far side and alongside a deer-park fence. Continue to follow the path beside the deer fence up over the rise and then down through a wood to the driveway to Woldingham School in the bottom of the next valley. Cross the driveway and carry on ahead up the tarmac bridleway past Deer Park House and between the former stables of Marden Park Farm. Here, turn left onto the outward route back over the railway and along Church Road to the start.

◀ Looking past Marden Park Farm into Marden Park

Limpsfield and The Chart

Distance 7km **Time** 2 hours
Terrain woodland, commons and lanes
Map OS Explorer 147 **Access** bus to
Limpsfield from Oxted

Another undulating route leads through woods and heathland from a picturesque village and church.

The walk starts in the village of Limpsfield, where there is parking on the High Street (or at New Road car park a little way along the route). St Peter's Church is known for its musical associations, not least because the composer Frederick Delius is buried here. Nearby Limpsfield Chart, or The Chart, also has artistic connections. It was the home of the literary couple Constance and Edward Garnett. Their home, The Cearne, was visited by many famous authors, including Joseph Conrad, Ford Madox Ford, D H Lawrence, Arthur Rackham, G B Shaw, and H E Bates.

Constance Garnett herself is best known for her translations into English, some 70 volumes in all, of works by Tolstoy, Chekhov, Pushkin and Gogol.

Head up the High Street, cross the A25 Westerham Road by the traffic lights and take the footpath on the opposite side up into woodland. After 50m fork left up to and across New Road, where there is a car park. Follow the footpath out of the rear of the car park onto Limpsfield Common, across a clearing, and bear right down a shallow dip and up to the junction of Brick Kiln Lane with Stoneswood Road.

Here, you join the Greensand Way which heads along Brick Kiln Road for just under 100m and then forks left through trees, over Chapel Road and along a fenced section to Pastens Road. Turn left past the houses of Pains Hill to a junction after 300m where you turn left with the Greensand Way up the driveway past cottages and through a patch of woodland

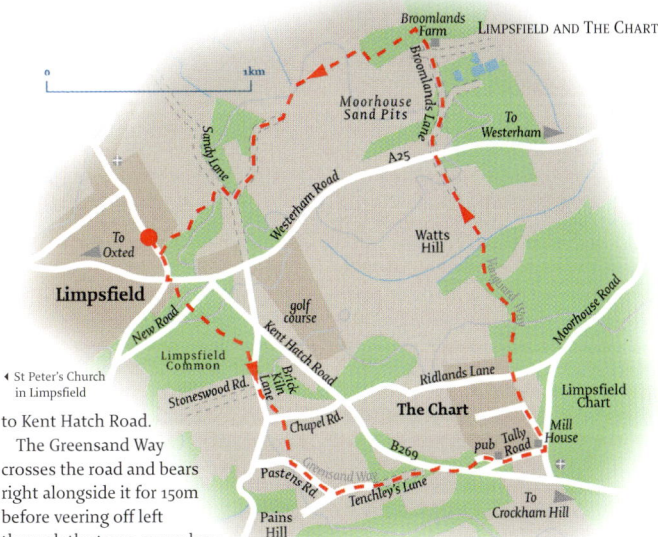

◀ St Peter's Church in Limpsfield

to Kent Hatch Road.

The Greensand Way crosses the road and bears right alongside it for 150m before veering off left through the trees, over a lane and past houses along Post Office Row in Limpsfield Chart. Bear right to Tally Road by The Carpenters Arms and turn left up to the junction with Moorhouse Road by The Mill House.

Leave the Greensand Way here and turn left onto the Vanguard Way, immediately forking left down Stoneleigh Road. At the bend the Vanguard Way keeps ahead on the bridleway which passes along the edge of the cricket field and over Ridlands Lane into woodland. Continue northwards down through the trees to a gate at the bottom of the wood. The Vanguard Way crosses two fields and the A25 beyond. Carry on ahead up Broomlands Lane, over a rise and down past Moorhouse Sand Pits to Broomlands Farmhouse.

Keep ahead into woodland and, after another 100m, leave the Vanguard Way and turn left onto a footpath up a woodland track to a bend, where you can glimpse the extensive pits on the left. A dogleg right for 50m round the bend, then left now takes you onto a narrower path through a strip of woodland for 100m, where you fork right to a field gate.

Descend the left-hand field edge beyond, with views across the valley and the M25 to Titsey Hill, before going left up the right-hand side of a second field to a gate into woodland. Head through the trees to the top of a lane, which takes you down past cottages and through bends to reach the edge of a golf course and a junction of paths. Here, dogleg right down Sandy Lane bridleway for 100m, then left onto a second bridleway along the bottom edge of woodland which returns you to Limpsfield in 500m.

Dormansland and Dry Hill

Distance 10km **Time** 2 hours 45
Terrain lanes, fields and woods
Map OS Explorer 147 **Access** bus to
Dormansland from Lingfield and
East Grinstead

Tucked away in the southeastern corner of the Surrey Hills is the lovely patchwork farmland around Dry Hill.

The walk starts from the top end of the village of Dormansland near the church and the pub, The Royal Oak. Dormansland lies in an outlying pocket of the Surrey Hills Area of Outstanding Natural Beauty, near the county border with Kent and East Sussex. The route's high point is Dry Hill, where you can see the earthworks of an extensive hillfort, excavated in the 1930s and shown to be pre-Roman.

Walk down the High Street from the pub and village stores, past the junction with The Meades, for 50m. Turn right onto a footpath along a driveway and then bear left along a fenced path between houses, over a rise and down to Hollow Lane. The footpath continues across the lane down through woodland and along the field edge to a gate down to the driveway by North Lodge.

A right turn along the driveway takes you up over a rise and down past the entrance to Greathed Manor. Keep ahead through the bends and where the drive bends right to The Courtyard (Dairy Farm House on the OS) fork left onto a bridleway track. The bridleway bends left, then right past a workshop, before rising gently up past a cottage through woodland and then between fields, over the rise and down to Littleworth Cottage. At the bend just beyond, turn right onto the route of the Tandridge Border Path and Vanguard Way along a bridleway which heads up between fields and then through Reynolds Wood, where it zigzags its way up to a bridleway junction.

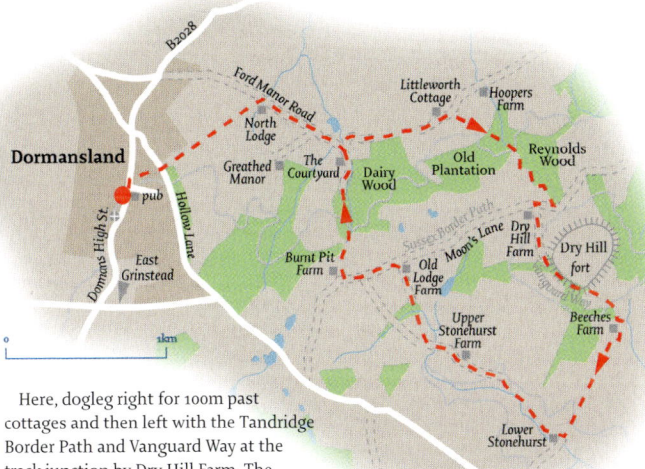

Here, dogleg right for 100m past cottages and then left with the Tandridge Border Path and Vanguard Way at the track junction by Dry Hill Farm. The bridleway rises between fields and then around the earthworks of Dry Hill fort, which now houses a covered reservoir, constructed in the early 20th century and enclosed by railings. Carry on over the rise past the triangulation pillar in the field on the left and descend with good views south down into a wood to Beeches Farm, where the bridleway doglegs left, then right around the farm buildings.

Here, you leave the Tandridge Border Path and Vanguard Way bridleway and turn right onto a footpath past Beeches Cottage, bearing left down the edges of two fields to a footpath junction near Lower Stonehurst Farm. Turn right past the outbuildings, beyond which the footpath heads between the stream on the left and fields to the right, before climbing the right-hand edge of two fields to Upper Stonehurst Farm. At the driveway bear left for 200m round the bend down into the dip and turn right onto the Sussex Border Path. This footpath heads across a field beside a stream before making its way up through woodland and along a narrow hedged section beside a fence to the lane by Old Lodge Farm.

A left turn, off the Sussex Border Path, along the lane for 350m takes you to Burnt Pit Farm, where a bridleway heads off right down through woodland and joins a track to The Courtyard. At the bend beyond, you turn left onto the outward route and follow the driveway back over the rise to North Lodge, where a final left turn takes you back up the field and into Dormansland.

◀ The view across fields east of Dormansland

Index

Alfold	42	Mole Valley	64
Betchworth	70	Newlands Corner	52
Bishop's Palace	8	Norbury Park	64
Black Down	40	North Downs Way	10, 28, 48, 52, 66, 82, 90
Box Hill	68		
Brockham	70	Peaslake	54
Chart, The	92	Peper Harow	16
Chiddingfold	38	Pilgrims Way	48
Chilworth	48	Pitch Hill	54
Chinthurst Hill	50	Puttenham	14
Churt	22	Ranmore Common	66
Colley Hill	82	Reigate	82, 84
Compton	28	St Martha's Hill	48
Crooksbury Hill	10	St Swithun's Way	8
Devil's Punch Bowl, The	24	Seale	12
Dockenfield	20	Serpent Trail	40
Dormansland	94	Shackleford	16
Dry Hill	94	Sheepleas	46
Eashing	30	Shere	52
Ewhurst	58	Sidney Wood	42
Farnham	8	Skimmington	84
Farthing Downs	86	Squire's Great Wood	72
Frensham	18, 20	Sussex Border Path	40, 94
Friday Street	76	Tandridge Border Path	94
Gibbet Hill	24	Temple of the Winds	40
Godalming	30	Thursley	24
Godstone	88	Tilburstow Hill	88
Greensand Way	36, 54, 56, 70, 72, 76, 88, 92	Tilford	18
		Vanguard Way	92, 94
Hambledon	36	Walliswood	60
Happy Valley	86	Watts Gallery Artists' Village	28
Hascombe	34	Waverley Abbey	10
Haslemere	40	Westcott	72
Hog's Back, The	12, 14	Westhumble	64, 66
Holmbury Hill	56	West Horsley	46
Holmwood Common	74	Wey South Path	42, 50
Hydon's Ball	36	Whitmoor Vale	22
Leith Hill	76, 78	Witley	32
Limpsfield	92	Woldingham	90
Loseley Park	28	Wonersh	50
Marden Park	90		